MARYLAND PATRIOTS

Their Lives, Contributions, and Burial Sites

JOE FARRELL • LAWRENCE KNORR • JOE FARLEY

Mechanicsburg, PA USA

Published by Sunbury Press, Inc.
Mechanicsburg, Pennsylvania

www.sunburypress.com

Copyright © 2025 by Joe Farrell, Joe Farley, and Lawrence Knorr.
Cover Copyright © 2025 by Sunbury Press, Inc.

Sunbury Press supports copyright. Copyright fuels creativity, encourages diverse voices, promotes free speech, and creates a vibrant culture. Thank you for buying an authorized edition of this book and for complying with copyright laws by not reproducing, scanning, or distributing any part of it in any form without permission. You are supporting writers and allowing Sunbury Press to continue to publish books for every reader. For information contact Sunbury Press, Inc., Subsidiary Rights Dept., PO Box 548, Boiling Springs, PA 17007 USA or legal@sunburypress.com.

For information about special discounts for bulk purchases, please contact Sunbury Press Orders Dept. at (855) 338-8359 or orders@sunburypress.com.

To request one of our authors for speaking engagements or book signings, please contact Sunbury Press Publicity Dept. at publicity@sunburypress.com.

FIRST SUNBURY PRESS EDITION: February 2025

Set in Adobe Garamond | Interior design by Crystal Devine | Cover by Lawrence Knorr | Edited by the authors.

Publisher's Cataloging-in-Publication Data
Names: Farrell, Joe, author | Farley, Joe, author | Knorr, Lawrence, author.
Title: Maryland patriots : their lives, contributions, and burial sites / Joe Farrell Lawrence Knorr Joe Farley.
Description: First trade paperback edition. | Mechanicsburg, PA : Sunbury Press, 2025.
Summary: The individuals from Maryland who played prominent roles in the founding of the USA are detailed.
Identifiers: ISBN 979-8-88819-295-5 (softcover).
Subjects: HISTORY / United States / Revolutionary Period (1775-1800) | BIOGRAPHY & AUTOBIOGRAPHY / Political.

Designed in the USA
0 1 1 2 3 5 8 13 21 34 55

For the Love of Books!

Contents

Introduction v

Matthew Tilghman Father of the Revolution in Maryland 1
Abraham Baldwin The Founder of the University of Georgia 5
Edward Biddle Speaker of the Pennsylvania Assembly 10
Charles Carroll of Carrollton The Catholic Signer 16
Daniel Carroll A Catholic Patriot 23
Samuel Chase First to be Impeached 27
Elbridge Gerry Founder of Gerrymandering 32
John Hanson President of the United States in Congress Assembled 38
Daniel of St. Thomas Jenifer Elder Statesman 43
Thomas Johnson One of the Original Supremes 48
John Paul Jones "I have not yet begun to fight!" 53
Edward Langworthy An Orphaned Founder 61
Thomas Lynch South Carolina Son of Liberty 64
James McHenry Secretary of War 68
William Paca Master of Wye 75
Thomas Stone Pacificist Patriot 79

Sources 85
Index 88

Introduction

Welcome to *Maryland Patriots*. This work aims to examine the lives and contributions of the amazing men and women who using their courage and talents, established the country those of us who live here, and many who do not have come to love. Our original plan called for a four-volume series, with each covering approximately fifty Founders, and that goal remains. However, based on our research, we have found that adding volumes that examine specific states is beneficial. As a result, we published a volume titled *Pennsylvania Patriots* in 2019, and this volume encompasses patriots buried in Maryland and the District of Columbia. Other state books will follow.

Over the past decade, we have made trips to numerous cemeteries to produce twelve volumes of the popular Keystone Tombstones and two titled Gotham Graves. This series covering the Founders follows the same format of those works and involved more effort in both time and research. Our travels to visit the graves of those we have identified as Founders have taken us to more than the thirteen original states. Accessing information about some of the lesser-known individuals who made contributions to the creation of the United States at times has been challenging. We hope that our efforts in meeting those challenges will please our readers.

The first question we had to answer regarding this series was who to include. In other words, who qualifies to be considered a founder? The standard we settled on resulted in the inclusion of signers of either the Continental Association, the Declaration of Independence, the Articles of Confederation, or the Constitution. In addition, we have also identified non-signers of the above-referenced documents who made significant contributions to the creation of the United States of America. John Paul Jones, the naval hero, whose story is told in this volume, is an example of the latter group.

We all agree that our visits to the gravesites and the research on the Founders have been rewarding and educational. However, in some cases, the visits have been sobering, shocking, and shameful. The well-known Founders such as Washington, Jefferson, Hamilton, and Madison have been laid to rest in well-maintained graves accessible to the public. Unfortunately, this is not the rule. Too many of our nation's Founders are buried in neglected places and have been left unattended and thus are subject to decay. Some are inaccessible, and others cannot be located at all due to the development of the land and poor record keeping. One of our goals in doing this series and including photographs of the graves is to bring this problem to light and hopefully spurn action to address this issue before it is simply too late. Several of the patriots in this volume are in such a predicament. Charles Carroll of Carrolton and William Paca are located on private property and cannot be visited. Edward Langworthy, Thomas Lynch, Daniel of St. Thomas Jennifer, Edward Biddle, and John Hanson, a president of Congress, are lost to us. Either their graves have been destroyed, or the locations are now unknown.

Considering the condition of many of these graves, we have established a website, www.adoptapatriot.com, where one can find information on all the people we have identified as Founders. We continue to update this site as we come across new information. In addition, the website includes a Wall of Shame where we highlight those gravesites that we have concluded are in the worst shape due to neglect or are in remote difficult to reach locations or where the founder is under memorialized given their contributions to the nation. It is our sincere hope that many of these graves will be restored, renewed, or relocated.

One thing we have learned about the Founders in writing this series, and we are confident that most of them would agree with us, is that they were products of their times and not perfect nor infallible. They disagreed on many of the issues they faced, and none may have been as hotly debated as slavery. As a matter of fact, on our many trips, we have had some heated debates as to how the various Founders dealt with slavery on both public and personal levels. It is difficult to reconcile men who undertook a war against the most powerful army in the world, proclaiming that all men are created equal while, at the same time, many of these same men held other men, women, and children in bondage. The contradiction is obvious and quite difficult to excuse. Nevertheless, we have attempted

INTRODUCTION

to tell each founder's story truthfully and deal with the slavery issue on a case-by-case basis. There are several chapters in this volume, including those on Daniel of St. Thomas Jenifer and Matthew Tilghman, where we hope our readers will find that we have met that standard.

As the country nears the upcoming 250th anniversary of the Declaration of Independence, we view these volumes as timely reminders of the Founders' sacrifices and contributions to create this nation. We should never forget those who put their lives and fortunes on the line and succeeded in establishing the greatest country the world has ever known. We are inspired by the words of Marcus Cicero:

POOR IS THE NATION HAVING NO HEROES
SHAMEFUL THE ONE THAT HAVING THEM FORGETS

Matthew Tilghman
(1717–1790)

Father of the Revolution in Maryland

Buried at Rich Neck Manor,
Claiborne, Maryland.

Continental Association

Matthew Tilghman was a planter and attorney from the Eastern Shore of Maryland, who served in the First and Second Continental Congresses, and signed the Continental Association. Known as "The Patriarch of Maryland" and "The Father of the Revolution in Maryland," Tilghman was a prominent member of a ruling clique in Maryland that included his cousin, Edward Lloyd, and William Paca, with whom he was related by marriage. Tilghman is credited with guiding the transition of Maryland from the colonial proprietor to statehood.

Matthew Tilghman was born on February 17, 1717 or 1718, at the family's estate, "The Hermitage," on the Chester River, near Centreville, Queen Anne's County, Maryland, the youngest son of Richard Tilghman, a colonial politician known as "Colonel Richard," and his wife, Anna Maria (née Lloyd) Tilghman. The elder Tilghman was the justice of the Provincial Court from 1746 to 1766. The Tilghman family, through blood and marriage, is related to Charles Carroll, William Paca, and Edward Lloyd, all of the Continental Congress, and Rogers Brooke Taney, who served as Chief Justice of the US Supreme Court.

MARYLAND PATRIOTS

Matthew Tilghman

The family's plantation, "The Hermitage," was considered one of the greatest in Maryland. It was first settled by Matthew Tilghman's grandfather, Richard Tilghman "The Elder," who was a surgeon in the British Navy in London. He emigrated to Maryland in 1660 with his wife and two children. Here, Matthew was raised and educated by the Reverend Hugh Jones, the rector of the St. Stephen's Parish, in Cecil County, Maryland. In 1733, he went to live with his cousin, Matthew Tilghman Ward, at Ward's "Rich Neck Manor," near the village of Claiborne, Talbot County, Maryland. When "Colonel Richard" died in 1739, Tilghman inherited 2000 acres. Then, when Ward died without any direct descendants in 1741, Tilghman inherited his estate of 2000 acres and 100 slaves. He married his first cousin Anne Lloyd on April 6,

INTRODUCTION

1741, and the two resided at the manor. They had five children. Their oldest daughter, Margaret, married Charles Carroll. The other children were Matthew Ward, Richard, Lloyd, and Anna Maria. Richard was a major in the militia of Queen Anne's County during the Revolution. Anna Maria married her cousin, Tench Tilghman, an aide-de-camp to George Washington.

In 1741, Samuel Oglethorpe, the governor of Maryland, appointed Tilghman as a justice of the peace for Talbot County. He held this post until at least 1746. In 1751, he was elected to the Maryland House of Delegates, serving from 1751 to 1774. Beginning in 1773, Tilghman was the speaker of that body. During the Stamp Act controversy, Tilghman's loyalties first switched away from Lord Baltimore. He and his son-in-law, Charles Carroll, refused appointments to the Lordship's Council.

As the Revolution neared, Tilghman was the prominent leader in Maryland as a member of the committee of correspondence, chairman of the committee of safety, and president of the Annapolis Convention. He was then appointed to the Continental Congress in 1774 and led the Maryland delegation.

Tilghman went to Philadelphia with Samuel Chase, Robert Goldsborough, Thomas Johnson, and William Paca. All but Goldsborough signed the Continental Association in response to the Boston port controversy. Tilghman was sent to the Second Continental Congress while also dealing with the collapse of the colonial government in Maryland. He was president of the committee that drafted the new constitution for the state and was essentially the head of the new government in Maryland. Tilghman also supported the Declaration of Independence, voting for its final approval. However, on June 21, 1776, Tilghman returned to Maryland to attend to affairs there and missed the signing of the Declaration of Independence. Charles Carroll of Carrollton replaced him in that role.

Tilghman's focus was now on his home state of Maryland. In 1777, he was elected to the state senate, serving until 1783, the last three years as the president of that body. Tilghman retired from the senate in 1783, now in his mid-60s, to tend to his plantation at Rich Neck, which had expanded to over 8000 acres, including Sherwood Manor, acquired in 1771.

In 1784, Tilghman served as a representative to a meeting of the Protestant Episcopal Church. He died of a stroke on May 4, 1790, at

Rich Neck. Said one obituary, "In his public Sphere, he stood high in the Confidence of his Country; and, until Age and Infirmities pleaded for Retirement, his Life might be said to have been one continued Scene of Labour, and Usefulness, in its Service; while he was ever considered as one of the firmest and most zealous Advocates of civil and religious Liberty."

Tilghman was buried in the family plot of Rich Neck which still stands near Claiborne, Maryland. The authors were grateful to the current owners for the ability to visit and photograph the grave, which is on private property in a beautiful location along the Chesapeake Bay.

Matthew Tilghman's grave.

Abraham Baldwin
(1754–1807)

The Founder of the University of Georgia

Buried at Rock Creek Cemetery,
Washington, D.C.

U.S. Constitution

Abraham Baldwin, a native of Connecticut, was a minister, lawyer, signer of the U.S. Constitution, congressman, senator, and founder of the University of Georgia.

Abraham Baldwin was born November 22, 1754, in North Guilford, Connecticut, the son and one of five children of Michael Baldwin, a blacksmith, and his wife, Lucy (née Dudley) Baldwin. Lucy died in childbirth with the fifth child when Abraham was four. Michael was a single parent for ten years until he married Theodora Wolcott, with whom he had seven additional children, including Henry Baldwin, who became a supreme court justice.

Michael worked hard to support his large family and borrowed money to provide secondary education for young Abraham. Baldwin attended Guilford Grammar School and then Yale College in 1768 when he was 14. He was a member of the secret Linonian Society, graduating in 1772. Baldwin studied theology in preparation to become a Congregationalist minister. In 1775, he was given a license to preach and was also hired as a teacher at Yale. During the early years of the Revolution, he served as

Abraham Baldwin

a tutor until 1779. In 1777, he enlisted as a chaplain in the Continental Army, serving with the Second Connecticut Brigade through 1783.

After the war, Yale president Ezra Stiles offered Baldwin the opportunity to be a professor of divinity, but he declined, instead pursuing law studies. He was encouraged by his former commanding officer General Nathanael Greene to follow him to Georgia, where Greene had a plantation. Baldwin did so and was admitted to the Georgia bar in 1783. Baldwin first practiced in Fairfield before moving to Augusta, Georgia. There, in 1785, he was elected to the Georgia House of Representatives where, at the urging of another transplanted New Englander, Lyman Hall, he focused on establishing an education system in the state. On

May 5, 1785, Baldwin was also elected to the Continental Congress and regularly attended, except 1786.

The first college established through Baldwin's legislative efforts in the Georgia House was Franklin College, now the University of Georgia. Baldwin served as its first president from 1786 to 1801 while the institution was being formed. Wrote biographer Henry Clay White,

> [Baldwin] came to Georgia seeking neither land nor fortune. He came as a missionary in the cause of education. Happily, we may well believe, his mission, for the moment, proved ill-timed. It was not abandoned but deferred, and, in the political service to which, he, perforce, was turned, he developed a genius which was of the inestimable benefit to his State and Country.

In 1787, Baldwin was appointed as a delegate to the Confederation Congress and then to the Constitutional Convention, along with William Few, William Pierce, George Walton, William Houston, and Nathaniel Pendleton. Baldwin was the most distinguished of the delegates. In September 1787 signed the U.S. Constitution. The Georgia Historical Society retains Baldwin's draft copy with his signature and handwritten notes.

Under the new government, Baldwin was elected to the U.S. House of Representatives in 1788, serving in the First Congress through the Fifth Congress from 1789 to 1799. He was then appointed by the Georgia legislature to the U.S. Senate and was re-elected in 1805 to a second six-year term. During his time in the Senate, from 1801 to 1803, he was the president pro tempore.

Back in Georgia, Franklin College finally had its first students in 1801. At that point, Baldwin resigned as president, and fellow Yale graduate Josiah Meigs took his place. The college buildings had been modeled after their alma mater, and the bulldog was adopted as the mascot, also borrowed from Yale.

On March 4, 1807, while serving as a U.S. senator from Georgia, Baldwin died. His remains were first in Rock Creek Cemetery, Washington, D.C., beside his colleague, Senator James Jackson. They

The grave of Abraham Baldwin

were then transferred to Kalorama, another area within D.C., and finally again to Rock Creek, just down the slope from the famous Saint Gaudens' figure.

Wrote historian Ralph D. Smith in 1877,

> It is a remarkable circumstance, and an instance of assiduity almost without parallel that, during his long congressional life, he was never known to be absent a single hour during the session of congress [sic], on account of disposition or any other cause, until the week preceding his death. He was a man of great industry and talents, and his distinguished patriotism, learning, and public

services shed an honor on his active state as well as that of his adoption.

The *Georgia Historical Quarterly* concluded in 1919,

> During the violent agitation of parties which have disturbed the repose of public men in this country for the last ten years, [Baldwin] has always been moderate but firm; relaxing nothing in his republican principles but retaining all possible charity for his former friends who may have abandoned theirs. He has lived without reproach and has probably died without an enemy.

Abraham Baldwin has been honored in many ways. Baldwin counties in Georgia and Alabama are named after him. His name also adorns Abraham Baldwin Agricultural College in Tifton, Georgia, and Abraham Baldwin Middle School in Guilford, Connecticut. There are Baldwin streets in Madison, Wisconsin, and Athens, Georgia. A statue of Baldwin was erected on the campus of the University of Georgia, and the U.S. Postal Service issued a stamp in his honor as part of the Great Americans series.

Edward Biddle
(1738–1779)

Speaker of the Pennsylvania Assembly

Buried at St. Paul's Cemetery,
Baltimore, Maryland

Continental Association

Edward Biddle, a native of Pennsylvania, represented that state in the First and Second Continental Congresses and signed the Continental Association. He was connected via marriage to the Ross family of Philadelphia and an uncle of Richard and Nicholas Biddle.

Edward Biddle was born in 1738 in Philadelphia, Pennsylvania, one of ten children of William Biddle (1698-1756) and his wife, Mary (née Scull) Biddle (1709-89). William's grandparents, William and Sarah Kempe Biddle, were Quakers who emigrated from Birlingham Parish, Worcester, England, in 1681 and settled in Mount Hope, New Jersey. Mother Mary was the daughter of Nicholas Scull, the surveyor-general of Pennsylvania.

Edward's father moved to Philadelphia before Edward's birth. Edward's brothers were Judge James Biddle, President Judge of the first judicial district, Commodore Nicholas Biddle, and Charles Biddle, Vice-President of the Supreme Executive Council of Pennsylvania.

Biddle's education was in the common schools, studying Latin and other languages, literature, philosophy, and other subjects. He

Edward Biddle (1738–1779)

Edward Biddle

then attended the Academy of Philadelphia (now the University of Pennsylvania) from 1752 to 1755, working as a tutor in English for a while.

With the outbreak of the French and Indian War in 1754, Biddle joined the Pennsylvania militia as an ensign. He wrote a letter to his father in Philadelphia, describing the alarm in Reading on November 16, 1755,

> My Dearest Father:—I am in so much horror and confusion I scarcely know what I am writing. The drum is beating to arms and bells ringing and all the people under arms. Within these two hours, we have had different though too certain accounts all

corroborating with each other, and this moment is an express arrived, dispatched by Michael Reis, at Tulpehocken, eighteen miles above this town, who left about thirty of their people engaged with about an equal number of Indians at the Reis'. This exclaim against the Quakers and some are scarcely restrained from burning the houses of those few who are in this town. Oh, my country! My bleeding country! I commend myself to the divine God of armies. Give my dutiful love to my dearest mother and my best love to brother Jemmy.

I am, honored sir, your most affectionate and obedient son,

E. Biddle.

Sunday, 1 o'clock. I have rather lessened than exaggerated our melancholy account.

Biddle served for the duration of the war, present at the taking of Forts Duquesne and Niagara. He was promoted to captain in 1763 and received five thousand acres of land for his service.

Biddle, at 23, married Elizabeth Ross on June 6, 1761. The couple had two daughters, Abigail and Catherine, who lived to adulthood. Elizabeth was the sister of George Ross, who was later a delegate to the Continental Congress and signer of the Declaration of Independence. The famed seamstress Betsy Ross was the wife of Elizabeth's nephew.

After Biddle returned from the war, he read law at the offices of George Ross. By 1767, Biddle was admitted to the bar, and the couple moved to Reading, Pennsylvania, where he practiced law. In 1768, Biddle was elected to the American Philosophical Society. He also became interested in politics and was elected to represent Berks County in the Pennsylvania Provincial Assembly, serving until that body was abolished during the Revolution and then the rebel assembly. Biddle drafted legislation to remove settlers from land that had not yet been purchased from the Indians and lobbied against taxation without representation from Britain by drafting petitions to King George III. He was elected the 28th Speaker on October 14, 1774, replacing James Galloway. Biddle served on seven committees, including the Committee of Correspondence.

Edward Biddle (1738–1779)

As the Revolution loomed, on July 22, 1774, the Pennsylvania Assembly sent a split delegation to the Continental Congress, including moderates Galloway, Humphreys, and Rhoads, and radicals Biddle, Mifflin, Morton, and Ross. Biddle attended sessions from September 5 to October 26, 1774. During his time in the Congress, Biddle was a member of the committee that drafted the Declaration of Rights and signed the Continental Association. He also oversaw the printing of the resolutions that passed Congress.

On January 23, 1775, Biddle traveled to Philadelphia from Reading. While crossing the Schuylkill River, he fell overboard into the ice-cold river. Forced to sleep in wet clothes, he caught cold and developed chronic rheumatism, leading to his deteriorating health and loss of sight in one eye. Biddle attended Congress from May 10 through July 1775 and signed the Olive Branch Petition. He did not attend Congress for the remainder of 1775 or during 1776.

Wrote John Adams to his wife, Abigail, on July 23, 1775,

> There is a young gentleman from Pennsylvania, whose name is Wilson, whose fortitude, rectitude, and abilities too, greatly outshine his master's. Mr. Biddle, the Speaker, has been taken off by sickness, Mr. Mifflin is gone to the camp, Mr. Morton is ill too so that this province has suffered by the timidity of two overgrown fortunes. The dread of confiscation or caprice, I know not what, has influenced them too much, yet they were for taking arms and pretended to be very valiant.

In a letter to fellow Connecticut delegate Joseph Trumbull, Silas Deane wrote in September 1775,

> The Congress is well-nigh full, little Business has yet been done, but This Week it will be seriously entered upon, and I wish in Vain, that Mr. [Thomas] Mifflin [of Pennsylvania] was here. Mr. Biddle continues dangerously ill, Mr. [James] Willson [sic; should be Wilson] at Fort Pitt on an Indian Treaty, and Mr. [Thomas] Willing [of Pennsylvania] a Constant attendant on Congress, will

give Mr. Mifflin a proper Idea of the representation of this Colony, to whom present my sincerest respects.

In his memoir, General James Wilkinson wrote,

> I took Reading in my route and passed some days in that place, where I had several dear and respected friends, and among them Edward Biddle, Esq., a man whose public and private virtues commanded respect and excited admiration from all persons; he was Speaker of the last Assembly of Pennsylvania under the Proprietary government, and in the dawn of the Revolution devoted himself to the cause of his country, and successfully opposed the overbearing influence of Joseph Galloway. Ardent, eloquent, and full of zeal, by his exertions during several days and nights of obstinate, warm, and animated discussion in extreme sultry weather, he overheated himself and brought on an inflammatory rheumatism and surfeit, which radically destroyed his health, and ultimately deprived society of one of its greatest ornaments, and his country of a statesman, a patriot, and a soldier; for he had served several campaigns in the war of 1756, and if his health had been spared would, no doubt, have occupied the second or third place in the revolutionary armies.

Back home, in Berks County, Biddle served on the Committee of Correspondence from 1774-1775 and the Committee of Observation and Inspection from 1774-1776. He was again appointed to serve in Congress in 1778 but declined due to rapidly failing health.

At only 41, Edward Biddle died in Chatsworth, Maryland, at his daughter's home near Baltimore, on September 5, 1779. He was buried in St. Paul's churchyard in Baltimore. Wrote a "Friend of Justice" in *The Pennsylvania Packet*, eulogizing Biddle, "The name of Col. Biddle will always be dear to those who knew the critical situation of our affairs in the year 1774. No difficulties or dangers appalled him. His eloquence in the counsels of our State, as well as in Congress, flashed like lightning with equal force upon the dignified Tory and temporizing Whig."

Edward Biddle (1738–1779)

Joseph Reed, President of the Supreme Executive Council for Pennsylvania, remarked,

> On Thursday last, after a very lingering illness, died at Baltimore, in the forty-first year of his age, that great lawyer, Hon. Edward Biddle, of Reading, in this State. In early life, as captain in our provincial forces, his military virtues so highly distinguished him that Congress designed him to high rank in the American army, which, however, his sickness prevented; his practice at the bar for years having made his great abilities and integrity known, the county of Berks unanimously elected him one of their representatives in Assembly, who soon made him their speaker and a delegate in Congress, and the conduct of the patriot did honor to their choice. As a public character, very few were equal to him in talents or noble exertion of them, so in private life, the son, the husband, the father, brother, friend and neighbor, and master had in him a pattern not to be excelled. Love to his country, benevolence, and every manly virtue rendered him an object of esteem and admiration to all that knew him.

Charles Carroll of Carrollton
(1737–1832)

The Catholic Signer

Buried at Doughoregan Manor Chapel,
Ellicott City, Maryland

Continental Congress • Declaration of Independence

Though born into one of the wealthiest families in America, this founder had to overcome religious intolerance to take his place among the signers of the document that declared the thirteen colonies independent. Born in Maryland, which was initially founded as a Catholic colony and named after a Catholic queen, by the time this founder entered the world, there were restrictions against Catholics prohibiting those of that faith to practice law, teach or hold public office. Despite these obstacles, this founder, with the aid of the family fortune, received a classical education in France, where he became fluent in that language. A gifted writer, his well-framed arguments against British rule earned him the respect of his fellow patriots. He was instrumental in persuading Maryland to give the colony's delegates to the Continental Convention the instructions to vote for independence. He would later rally the state's support for the Constitution and serve as one of Maryland's first United States senators. When he passed away at the age of 95, he was the last surviving signer of the Declaration of Independence. His name was Charles Carroll, but his signature generally read Charles Carroll of Carrollton.

Charles Carroll of Carrollton (1737–1832)

Charles Carroll of Carrollton

Carroll was born on September 19, 1737, in the Carroll Mansion located in Annapolis, Maryland. He was the only child of Charles Carroll of Annapolis and Elizabeth Brooke. His father was a wealthy tobacco farmer. Carroll was educated at a Jesuit preparatory school until the age of eleven, when he was sent to France to continue his studies. Among the French schools he attended was the Louis the Great College in Paris, from which he graduated in 1755. For the next decade, he continued his studies in France, becoming fluent in the French language before studying the law in England. He returned to America in 1765 as an intelligent and cultured young gentleman.

Initially, upon returning to the land of his birth, Carroll showed little interest in politics. This lack of interest may have been abetted by a Maryland law passed in 1704 that prohibited Catholics from holding public office to prevent "the growth of Popery in the Province." Also, as detailed by Milton Lomask in his book *Charles Carroll and the American Revolution,* Carroll's father urged him to be cautious in addressing the political issues of the day, especially the increasing tensions between Great Britain and the colonies. He did marry during this period wedding Mary (Molly) Darnell, on June 5, 1768. The couple would have seven children before Mary's death in 1782, but only three would survive infancy.

By 1772 Carroll's reluctance to engage in political debates had vanished. He engaged in what Denise Kieran and Joseph D'Agnese described as "a duel of pens" in their work *Signing Their Lives Away: The Fame and Misfortune of the Men Who Signed the Declaration of Independence.* In this "duel," which began with both participants writing under pseudonyms, Carroll was pitted against a well-known Maryland Attorney and crown loyalist Daniel Dulany the Younger. The subject of their debate was the decision by the proprietary governor to raise taxes so that government officials could receive a pay raise. Dulany supported the governor, while Carroll viewed the move as further taxation without representation. After a series of their arguments were published in a newspaper, word spread as to the true identities of the authors. Dulany began attacking Carroll personally, stressing the fact that he was a Catholic. Carroll's responses to these personal attacks were careful and restrained. He wrote that his opposition had resorted to "virulent and illiberal abuse," adding that "we may fairly presume, that arguments are either wanting, or that ignorance or incapacity know not how to apply them." Dulany's personal attacks backfired, resulting in Carroll being recognized as a strong and leading opponent of British rule.

While Carroll may have risen to patriotic prominence through his pen, he was one of the initial founders who came to believe that the disputes with England would have to be settled by the sword. Legend has it that in a conversation with Samuel Chase, another future signer of the Declaration of Independence, Carroll took the position that it would take more than written arguments if the colonies were to prevail over the British. When Chase asked what else the colonists could resort to, Carroll answered, "The bayonet. Our arguments will only raise the feelings of the people to that pitch when open war will be looked to as the arbiter of the dispute."

On October 19, 1774, Carroll played a prominent role in the event that came to be known as the Annapolis Tea Party. During this time, the colonists were engaged in widespread tea boycotts to protest the British Tea Act of 1773, which permitted only one company, the British East India Company, to sell tea in the colonies without paying tax. These protests had already led to the more famous Boston Tea Party. As a result of the boycotts, most ship captains refused to transport tea. However, in 1774 an English merchant loaded a ton of tea aboard a ship called the *Peggy Stewart*. The ship arrived in Annapolis on October 14, 1774. The co-owner of the ship, Anthony Stewart, was notified of the tax that needed to be paid before any of the ship's cargo could be brought ashore. The cargo included 53 indentured servants who had already endured a harsh crossing and were unlikely to survive a forced return to England. Seeing no other alternative, Stewart guaranteed payment of the tax, got the servants ashore but left the tea on the ship while he met with the local committee that supervised the boycott to resolve the situation.

Stewart met with Carroll, who was chairman of the committee, and an agreement was reached that the tea would be burned and Stewart and his co-owners would publish an apology in the *Maryland Gazette*. On the morning of the 19th, the ship's crew ran her aground. Stewart arrived and, before a large crowd touched a torch to oil-soaked rags in the bow of the *Peggy Stewart*. The ship, tea and all, burned down to the waterline. According to Lomask, after the event, Carroll told his wife, "You must admit that when we hold a tea party here in Annapolis, we do a better job of it than they do in Boston. We do not disguise ourselves as Indians. We do not hide behind war paint and feathers. And we do not lay hands on property that is not ours. We do everything legally and openly - and in a grand manner."

By the time the American Revolution began in 1775, Carroll was one of the colonies' wealthiest men. He inherited enormous agricultural estates, and his personal fortune was 2.1 million pounds sterling, which would amount to over $250 million today. He lived on and ran a ten-thousand-acre estate in Maryland that was worked by approximately 1,000 African slaves.

Carroll became a member of the first Annapolis Committee of Safety in 1775 and served as a delegate to the Annapolis Convention, which ran Maryland's revolutionary government. He was asked to represent his colony in the First Continental Congress but declined, probably believing that his Catholic faith would create problems for the representatives from other colonies. He did accompany Maryland's representatives to Philadelphia as an unofficial member of the delegation.

Though not an official member Congress soon found work for Carroll to do. In 1776 largely due to Benjamin Franklin and Samuel Chase's influence, Carroll was persuaded to head a mission to Canada to convince that country to join the fight against the British. Sending the Catholic French-speaking Carroll to Catholic-heavy Canada seemed a wise choice, but the effort came to naught for several reasons. Most notably, the Americans had invaded Canada less than a year earlier, and in 1774 the British parliament had passed the Quebec Act giving freedom of religion to Canadians and recognizing the Catholic Church. The First Continental Congress, despite Carroll's protests, had criticized the parliament for passing the act. The Canadians felt they had more to fear from their southern neighbors than from the British crown.

In the summer of 1776, Congress scheduled a vote for July 2 on Richard Henry Lee's resolution calling for American independence. Maryland had yet to advise their delegates on how to vote on the resolution, so Carroll and his old friend Samuel Chase headed back to Maryland to work the Annapolis Convention to support independence. Their arguments proved persuasive, and the convention freed Maryland delegates to support the Lee resolution. On July 4, 1776, Carroll was elected to the Continental Congress, and this time he agreed to serve. He arrived back in Philadelphia too late to vote in favor of independence, but he proudly signed the document that declared the American colonies free of English rule on August 2, 1776. He signed as Charles Carroll of Carrollton. There are stories about this signature, most likely apocryphal. In the 1940s, there was a journalist with a popular syndicated column named John Hix. He wrote in his column "Strange As It Seems" an explanation for Carroll's distinctive signature. Every member of the Continental Congress who signed this document automatically became a criminal, guilty of sedition against King George III. Because of his wealth, Carroll had more to lose than most yet had a very common name. Those signers with common names might hope to avoid being identified by the King. According to Hix's research, when it was Carroll's turn to sign the declaration, he rose, went to John Hancock's desk where the document rested, signed his name "Charles Carroll," and returned to his seat. At this point, another member of the Continental Congress, who was prejudiced against Carroll because of his Catholicism, commented that Carroll risked little in signing the document as there must be many men named Charles Carroll in the colonies so the King would be unlikely to order Carroll's arrest without clear proof that he was the same one who signed. Carroll immediately returned to Hancock's desk, seized the pen again, and added "of Carrollton" to his name. The Society of the Descendants of the Signers of the Declaration of Independence claims that John Hancock made the comment.

Carroll would represent Maryland in the Continental Congress until 1778. He was a major supporter of George Washington as the two had become friends when the future president made multiple visits to the Carroll estate. He served on the committee that visited Washington and his troops during the harsh winter they spent at Valley Forge. He played a significant role in defeating the Conway Cabal that sought to replace Washington as commander of the new nation's armies. During his final year in Congress, he was asked to serve as President, an honor he declined. He also provided considerable financial support to the Revolutionary War effort throughout these turbulent times.

Carroll returned to Maryland in 1778 to assist in the formation of a state government. Since he had assisted in drafting the state constitution two years prior, he was well prepared for this task. He was elected to the state senate in 1781, where he served for more than a decade. He was elected to represent his state at the Constitutional Convention of 1787 but did not attend the gathering in Philadelphia. He was active in rallying support for ratification of the historical document produced by that convention. In 1789 he was elected to serve as one of Maryland's first two United States Senators. In 1792 the Maryland legislature passed a law prohibiting anyone from serving in the state and national legislature at the same time. Preferring service in the Maryland Senate, he resigned from the United States Senate in November of 1792.

Like many of the nation's founders, Carroll was a slave owner who wrestled with the question of slavery through much of his life. While he supported the gradual abolition of slavery and said, "It is admitted by all to be a great evil," he did not free any of his slaves. He did introduce a bill calling for the gradual abolition of slavery in the Maryland Senate, but it found little support. In 1828, when he was 91 years old, he served as the president of the Auxiliary State Colonization Society of Maryland. This group supported sending black Americans to lead free lives in African states such as Liberia.

When John Adams and Thomas Jefferson both passed away on July 4, 1826, Carroll became the last surviving founder of those who had courageously signed the Declaration of Independence. He lived his final years with a daughter in Baltimore. His last public act, on July 2, 1828, was the laying of the cornerstone of the B&O's Carrollton Viaduct, named in his honor and still in use today. In May 1832, he was asked to appear at the first-ever Democratic Party Convention but did not attend because of poor health. He passed away at the age of 95 on November 14, 1832. He was laid to rest in his Doughoregan Manor Chapel located in Ellicott City, Maryland.

There are numerous cities and counties named in his honor, and his family manors remain standing. The family still owns Doughoregan Manor, although it is closed to the public. There are numerous memorials to Charles Carroll throughout the eastern United States. Counties in twelve states bear his name, as do elementary and middle schools and a residence hall at the University of Notre Dame. His likeness can be found in many paintings depicting the Signers of the Declaration of Independence, and a statue of him resides in Statuary Hall in the US Capitol.

Daniel Carroll
(1730–1796)
A Catholic Patriot

Buried at St. John the Evangelist Church Cemetery,
Forest Glen, Maryland.

Articles of Confederation • U.S. Constitution

Daniel Carroll was a politician from Maryland and one of our Founding Fathers. He was a prominent member of one of the United States' great colonial Catholic families, whose members included his younger brother, Archbishop John Carroll, the first Roman Catholic bishop in the United States and founder of Georgetown University; and their cousin Charles Carroll of Carrollton, who signed the Declaration of Independence. Daniel was reluctant at first to get involved in the patriot cause because he was concerned that the Revolution might fail and as a rich slaveholder and large landowner he would be ruined. He gradually got over this fear and joined the cause to become one of five men to sign both the Articles of Confederation and the Constitution.

Daniel Carroll was born on July 22, 1730, in Upper Marlboro, Maryland to a wealthy family. He spent his early years at "Darnall's Chance," a plantation of 27,000 acres which his mother Eleanor Darnall Carroll had inherited from her grandfather. Several acres of this estate are now a museum and it is listed in the National Register of Historic Places. Between 1742 and 1748 he studied at the College of St. Omer in French

Portrait of Daniel Carroll etched by Albert Rosenthal, 1888, based on a photograph of a painting.

Flanders, a Jesuit school established for the education of English Catholics. He then went on a tour of Europe and returned home where he soon married Eleanor Carroll, a first cousin of Charles Carroll of Carrollton.

For about the next 20 years Carroll was slowly and gradually converting to the patriot cause. He believed that if the colonists failed in their effort to win their independence he would face financial ruin.

Catholics were prohibited from holding office at that time by colonial laws. After the laws were nullified in 1776 by the Maryland Constitution, Carroll was elected to the Maryland Senate and served from 1777 to 1781. As a state senator, he helped raise troops and money for the American cause.

He was then elected to the Continental Congress and served there from 1781 until 1784. In 1781 towards the end of the Revolution, he signed the Articles of Confederation, which formally established the United States.

In 1787 Carroll was named a Maryland delegate to the Philadelphia Convention which convened to revise the Articles of Confederation and produced the Constitution. He had become good friends with both George Washington and James Madison and like them believed that a strong central government was needed to regulate commerce among the states and with other nations. He wanted the power of the government to be vested in the people. He served on the Committee on Postponed Matters and spoke about 20 times in the debates at the Convention. He spoke out repeatedly in opposition to the payment of members of Congress by the states and when it was suggested that the president should be elected by Congress, Carroll moved that the words "by the legislature" be replaced with "by the people". He was the author of the presumption–enshrined in the Constitution—that powers not specifically delegated to the federal government were reserved to the states or to the people. Carroll and Thomas Fitzsimons were the only Catholics to sign the Constitution but their signing was a symbol of the advance of religious freedom in America.

After the convention, he returned to Maryland and campaigned for ratification but was not a delegate to the Maryland state convention. He defended the Constitution in the *Maryland Journal*, often in opposition to the arguments of the well-known Maryland anti-Federalist Samuel Chase. He ended one of his letters to the paper by saying "Regarding it then in every point of view with a candid and disinterested mind I am bold to assert that it is the best form of government which has ever been offered to the world." After the Constitution was ratified, Carroll was elected to the First Congress of 1789, meeting in New York City and representing the Sixth Congressional District of Maryland. There he voted for the assumption of state debts accumulated during the war by the federal government. This was part of a "grand bargain" proposed by the U.S. Secretary of the Treasury Alexander Hamilton and agreed to by Secretary of State Thomas Jefferson. Part of the bargain was the locating of the new national capital in the upper South along the Potomac River.

MARYLAND PATRIOTS

In 1791, George Washington named his friend Daniel Carroll as one of three commissioners to survey and define the District of Columbia, where Carroll owned much land. The new United States Capitol was to be built on the wooded hill owned by his nephew. As one of his first official acts as commissioner, on April 15, 1791, he and David Stuart of Virginia, a fellow commissioner laid the cornerstone for the beginning boundary line of the District at Jones Point, on the south bank of the Potomac. He served as a commissioner until 1795, when he retired because of poor health.

In the last year of Carroll's life, he became a partner with George Washington in their Patowmack Company. The intent of this company was to link the middle states with the west by means of a Potomac River canal. Daniel Carroll died on May 7, 1796, at the age of 65 at his home in the present village of Forest Glen. He was interred at St. John the Evangelist Catholic Cemetery there.

The grave of Daniel Carroll at St. John the Evangelist Catholic Church Cemetery in Forest Glen, Maryland (photo by Lawrence Knorr).

Samuel Chase
(1741–1811)

First to be Impeached

Buried at Old St. Paul's Cemetery,
Baltimore, Maryland.

**Continental Association • Declaration of Independence
Supreme Court Justice**

In 1766 town officials in Annapolis, Maryland published an article in the *Maryland Gazette Extraordinary* that described one young citizen as "a busy, restless incendiary, a ringleader of mobs, a foul-mouthed and inflaming son of discord and faction, a common disturber of the public tranquility, and a promoter of the lawless excesses of the multitude." The man who may well have embraced the description would later serve in the Continental Congress, sign the Declaration of Independence, and serve as an Associate Justice on the United States Supreme Court. Born on April 17, 1741, his name was Samuel Chase.

Chase's background and upbringing were not what one would expect of a fiery revolutionary. His father was an Episcopalian clergyman who moved to what was then the village of Baltimore to minister to the congregation of St. Paul's Church. His mother, Matilda, passed away soon after giving birth to the couple's only son. Chase was homeschooled by his father before leaving for Annapolis to study law. He was admitted to the bar in 1761. He started a law practice and soon earned the reputation

Portrait of Samuel Chase, circa 1811, by John Wesley Jarvis.

of a man unafraid to speak his mind regardless of whom, including the rich and powerful, might be offended. He had a reddish-brown complexion that seemed to grow more colorful when he engaged in a debate or argument. This trait earned him the nickname "Bacon Face."

In 1762 Chase married Ann Baldwin and the couple had seven children though only four survived to adulthood. Ann passed away in 1776 and Chase remarried eight years later. The second Mrs. Chase was the daughter of an English physician and she bore the American patriot two daughters.

Chase got his start in politics when he was elected to the Maryland General Assembly in 1764. He was also active in a group known as the Sons of Liberty whose purpose was to protect American colonists from oppressive British laws. This was close to the heart of the young Chase. After the Stamp Act was passed in 1765, Chase led a group of fellow patriots on a raid of public offices in Annapolis where they destroyed the stamps and burned the tax collector in effigy. Criticized publicly by the Loyalist mayor for these acts, Chase responded in the newspaper where he admitted to taking part in the raid adding that he did so while others who shared his beliefs "meanly grumbled in your corners and not daring to speak your sentiments." He was 24 years old at the time.

Though he may not have been popular with local officials his reputation among patriots earned him an appointment to the First Continental Congress in 1774. When it came to the work of Congress, Chase was a popular member owing to his willingness to serve on multiple committees and his effectiveness in carrying out his duties. He remained a member of Congress until 1778.

In 1776 Chase returned from Canada with Charles Carroll and Benjamin Franklin after the trio had been unsuccessful in convincing those colonies to provide military support in the Revolutionary War. Back in Maryland, the legislature had yet to decide on how the state should vote on the question of American independence. Chase returned to his home state to lobby support for separation from England. Thanks in part to his efforts, Maryland instructed its delegation to vote in favor of independence.

Chase, much to his chagrin, was not present when the historic vote was taken. He remained in Maryland tending to his ailing wife until the middle of July. It wasn't until August 2, in what may well have been his proudest moment, that he was able to affix his signature to the Declaration of Independence.

In 1778 Chase left Congress after being discredited in newspapers for using inside information to profit from the wartime flour market. Returning to Maryland he made a number of bad investments that left him bankrupt. He went back to practicing law in order to remedy his financial situation.

In 1787 Chase declined an appointment to the Constitutional Convention. By this time he was leading a campaign in Maryland for paper money emission, a matter of vital importance when it came to his personal finances as a result of debts he had incurred while speculating on confiscated estates of those who had remained loyal to the English.

When the ratification of the Constitution was debated in Maryland, Chase, joined by fellow Declaration of Independence signer William Paca, opposed it. George Washington and James Madison used their influence in the state to overcome the objections raised by Chase and Paca.

After the Constitution was ratified Chase became a firm Federalist and supporter of the new government. On January 26, 1796, President Washington appointed Chase to the United States Supreme Court. Though he was now a member of the nation's highest court this exalted position did nothing to curb his tendency, some might say need, to express his views. Some held that he bullied defendants and their lawyers. Nor was he shy about continuing to express his political views.

When Thomas Jefferson was elected President in 1800, Chase was an unapologetic critic of the nation's new leader. He said that under

The worn tombstone of Samuel Chase at Old St. Paul's Cemetery in Baltimore, Maryland (photo by Lawrence Knorr).

Jefferson's leadership "our Republican Constitution will sink to mobocracy, the worst of all possible governments." Jefferson was determined to purge the judiciary of Federalist judges. Urged by the President, the House of Representatives impeached Chase for allegedly showing extreme partisan conduct while on the bench while deciding several cases. Chase was the first and only Supreme Court Justice ever impeached. His trial took place early in 1805 with the United States Senate presided over by then Vice President Aaron Burr sitting in judgment. Chase was acquitted of all charges in a case that many historians credit with ensuring the independence of the judiciary.

Chase was still serving on the court in 1811 when he suffered a heart attack and passed away. He was laid to rest In Baltimore's Old St. Paul's Cemetery. Though the cemetery has been designated as a historic site by the United States government it sits behind a locked fence and is overgrown and neglected. Were Chase alive today he would likely be quite outspoken and leading protests relative to the lack of care being shown to what should be a revered property.

Elbridge Gerry
(1744–1814)

Founder of Gerrymandering

Buried at Congressional Cemetery,
Washington, D.C.

Declaration of Independence • Articles of Confederation

Elbridge Gerry was a very important Founder of the United States. He signed the Articles of Confederation and the Declaration of Independence. He was a major figure at the Constitutional Convention speaking to the convention 153 times. He served as Governor of Massachusetts and as Vice President under James Madison. He was smart, well educated, hardworking, and tenacious. He was also regarded as annoying and not well-liked. He would, after addressing the convention 153 times and winning many debates and forcing many compromises, be one of only three men who attended the convention to refuse to sign the Constitution. He then went on to oppose ratification. The term "gerrymandering" was coined while he was governor of Massachusetts and approved a controversial redistricting plan that favored Republicans.

Gerry was born in 1744 at Marblehead, Massachusetts. He was the third of eleven children although only five survived to adulthood. The family was wealthy and Gerry was educated by tutors and entered Harvard just before turning fourteen. After receiving a B.A. in 1762 and an M.A. in 1765, he participated in his father's merchant business. He entered the

Elbridge Gerry (1744–1814)

Portrait of Elbridge Gerry by James Bogle after John Vanderlyn.

colonial legislature in 1772 where he worked closely with Samuel Adams. He, Adams, and Hancock served on the Council of Safety where Gerry raised troops and dealt with military logistics. On April 18, 1775, Gerry attended a council meeting at an inn between Lexington and Concord and barely escaped the British troops marching on those towns.

In 1774 he was elected to the First Continental Congress but refused to serve because he was grieving the recent loss of his father. In 1776 he served in the Second Continental Congress where he supported and signed the Declaration of Independence and later was a signer of the Articles of Confederation.

Well known for his personal integrity, Gerry felt strongly about and advocated regularly about limiting central government and civilian control of the military. He also opposed the idea of political parties. He felt so strongly about the issue of centralizing too much power that he resigned from the Continental Congress in protest in 1780. He rejoined Congress in 1783 and served until 1785. The next year he married Ann Thompson who was twenty years younger than him. James Monroe was his best man. The couple settled in Cambridge and had ten children between 1787 and 1801.

Gerry played a major role at the U.S. Constitutional Convention held in Philadelphia during the summer of 1787. He arrived in late May several weeks after it had begun. During June he frequently helped check the nationalists by arguing and voting against their motions. He forced them to give up on an absolute veto power for the chief executive and on giving the central government an absolute power to negate state laws.

Gerry advocated indirect elections believing people could be easily misled. He managed to obtain such elections for the Senate whose members were to be elected by state legislatures but was unsuccessful in the case of the House. He made numerous proposals for the indirect election of the chief executive which was somewhat achieved with the Electoral College.

By the end of June, the Convention was on the verge of collapse over the issue of the relationship of the central government to the states. On July 2, after a deadlocked vote on whether the states would be equally represented in the Senate, Gerry told his colleagues that if the Convention failed "we shall not only disappoint America but the rest of the world." A committee was appointed to produce a compromise and Gerry was appointed its chairman. A compromise on the issues was finally achieved which provided for proportional representation in the House and equal representation in the Senate and provided that the House would raise revenue and appropriate money. When Gerry presented the committee report to the full convention for approval he stated: "If we do not come to some agreement among ourselves, some foreign sword will probably do the work for us." On July 15, after ten more days of debate, it was put to a vote. It passed by a 5-4 margin. Gerry had played an important role at a critical juncture in the convention.

Once the convention moved on, Gerry was a strong advocate for issues he believed in. Between July 17 and July 26, he made twenty-nine speeches on the powers to be granted to the central government, the jurisdiction of the judiciary, and the election of the President. He opposed

Elbridge Gerry (1744–1814)

the Congress electing the President instead proposing that the governors select the electors who would elect the President. It was at his urging that the Convention adopted an impeachment provision. He was also successful in proposing that senators of a state vote as individuals rather than cast a single vote on behalf of the state which at that point was the assumption.

During the next six weeks, Gerry made seventy-eight speeches on such issues as limiting the power of the central government, preventing a peacetime standing army, limiting the size of the army, and empowering the President only to make war but not to declare war. He opposed having a Vice President, an office he would one day hold.

Gerry was unhappy about the lack of expression of any sort of individual liberties in the proposed Constitution. On September 17, he addressed the Convention for the one hundred fifty-third and last time stating he could not sign the document. He then watched as thirty-nine men signed it. Two others, Edmund Randolph and George Mason, also refused.

Gerry continued his opposition during the ratification debates that took place after the convention. He published a letter that was widely circulated documenting his objections. He cited the lack of a Bill of Rights as his primary objection. If the people adopted the document as it stood, they were in danger of losing their liberties. But if they rejected it altogether, anarchy may ensue. His opposition cost him a number of close political friends. Massachusetts ratified the Constitution but recommended amendments. Before the Massachusetts ratification convention, none of the states had requested amendments. After it, all but one ratified it with proposed amendments.

In 1789, after he announced his intention to support the Constitution, he was elected to the first Congress where he championed federalist policies. He proposed that Congress consider all the proposed constitutional amendments that various states had called for. He successfully lobbied for inclusion of freedom of assembly in the First Amendment and was a leading architect of the Fourth Amendment protections against search and seizure.

In 1793, after two terms in Congress, Gerry did not stand for re-election and returned home. His retirement from public service didn't last long as in 1797 President Adams appointed him to be a member of

The grave of Elbridge Gerry at Congressional Cemetery in Washington, D.C. (photo by Lawrence Knorr).

a special diplomatic commission sent to France to negotiate a reconciliation in hopes of avoiding a war. This episode became known as the XYZ Affair. The mission failed and Gerry's reputation was damaged.

Between 1800 and 1803 Gerry ran four times for the governorship of Massachusetts and lost each time. He tried again in 1810 and won. He repeated a victory in 1811. Both times he ran as a Republican. Near the

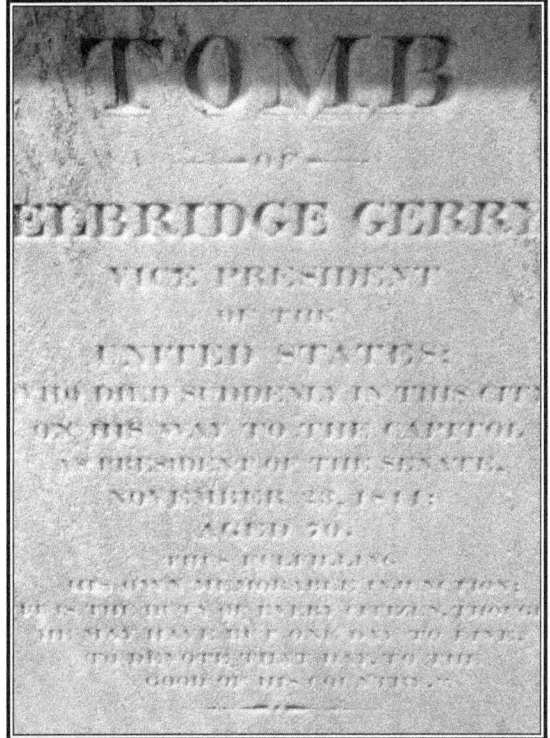

Detail of Gerry's tombstone (photo by Lawrence Knorr).

end of his second term, the Republicans passed a redistricting measure to ensure their domination of the state senate. This led to Federalists heaping ridicule on Gerry and they used the term "gerrymander" to describe the salamander shape of one of the new districts.

He was chosen to be James Madison's vice presidential running mate in 1812 and they easily won. On November 23, 1814, the seventy-year-old Gerry collapsed on his way to the Senate and died. He is buried in the Congressional Cemetery in Washington, D.C. He is depicted in two paintings, the "Declaration of Independence" and "General George Washington Resigning His Commission" both on view in the rotunda of the United States Capitol. He is also depicted in murals in the National Archives near displays of the Articles of Confederation, Declaration of Independence, Constitution, and Bill of Rights.

John Hanson
(1715–1783)

President of the United States in Congress Assembled

Buried at Addison Burial Ground,
Oxon Hill, Maryland

Articles of Confederation • President of Congress

John Hanson was a merchant and politician from Maryland who was a member of the Continental Congress. He signed the Articles of Confederation and was then elected the first President of Congress Assembled after their ratification.

John Hanson was born on April 3, 1715, at the plantation "Mulberry Grove" in Port Tobacco Parish, Charles County, Maryland, the son of Samuel Hanson (1685-1740), a planter, and his wife, Elizabeth (née Storey) Hanson (1688-1764). Samuel owned more than 1,000 acres and served in various political offices, including the Maryland General Assembly. Hanson's grandfather, also named John, was an indentured servant who came to Charles County, Maryland, circa 1661.

There is no record or mention of Hanson receiving formal schooling, so it is assumed by historians he was tutored privately, as was customary. He followed in his father's footsteps, managing the plantation. Circa 1744, Hanson married Jane Contee of a well-known Maryland family. She was only sixteen at the time, and the couple remained married for Hanson's entire life. The couple had nine children, five of whom lived to adulthood.

John Hanson (1715–1783)

John Hanson

Hanson's first political office was sheriff of Charles County in 1750. He then followed his father as the representative of Charles County in the Maryland General Assembly, serving for twelve years starting in 1757. During the 1760s, Hanson was a leading agitator against the Sugar Act of 1764 and the Stamp Act of 1765. In 1769, he signed the nonimportation resolution boycotting British imports in response to the Townshend Acts. At this time, Hanson resigned from the General Assembly, sold his Charles County properties, and moved to Frederick County, Maryland. There, he was elected deputy surveyor, sheriff, and county treasurer.

As tensions increased with Great Britain in 1774, Hanson became a leading patriot in Frederick County. He led the passage of a town resolution opposing the Boston Port Act and sent 200 pounds of his own money to support the citizens. The next year, he was a delegate to the Maryland Convention that replaced the General Assembly and was the Maryland Committee of Correspondence chairman. He signed the Association of Freeman on July 26, 1775, hoping for reconciliation, but calling for military resistance to the enforcement of the Coercive Acts.

Hanson was also highly active in organizing the local military, recruiting and arming soldiers, paying them with his own funds. Frederick County sent the first southern troops to join George Washington. They were led by Michael Cresap and Thomas Price, arriving in Boston on August 9, 1775, after marching twenty-two days. Hanson's son, Lieutenant Peter Contee Hanson, was among them. He was mortally wounded at Fort Washington and died in November 1775.

In June 1776, Hanson and his Frederick County patriots urged Maryland's delegates in the Continental Congress to declare independence from Britain. Meanwhile, Hanson was busy "making gunlocks, storing powder, guarding prisoners, raising money and troops, dealing with Tories, and doing the myriad other tasks which went with being chairman of the committee of observation."

In 1777, Hanson was elected to the new Maryland House of Delegates, serving five annual terms. In December 1779, they named him a delegate to the Second Continental Congress. Hanson began serving in Philadelphia in June 1780, immediately becoming involved in various finance committees. At the time, the ratification of the Articles of Confederation was stalled in Maryland because of concerns about western land claims. After the other states agreed to relinquish their western claims that interfered with Maryland, Hanson and Daniel Carroll signed the Articles on March 1, 1781. At this point, the Articles were officially ratified at the national level and went into effect.

Since its inception, the Continental Congress had a presiding officer titled the President of Congress who oversaw the debates and deliberations. Eight men had played this part in the early days of our nation. With the signing of the Articles of Confederation, the new office of President of the Congress Assembled was created as the first presiding officer of the officially united colonies. At that moment, Samuel Huntington, the incumbent President of Congress, transitioned from the prior role to the new one, but his term was now exceeding a year. On July 9, 1781, Samuel Johnston was the first man elected to the new office, but he declined. Thomas McKean was next elected but served only a few months, resigning after the surrender at Yorktown. On November 5, 1781, Congress elected Hanson as President of Congress Assembled, succeeding Thomas McKean. The role involved moderating discussions, handling official correspondence, and signing documents. Hanson did not enjoy the role out of the gate and discussed resigning after one week, citing his health and family responsibilities. His colleagues urged him to remain due to the lack of a quorum necessary to choose a successor. Hanson carried out his duty through his entire one-year term, ending November 4, 1782.

During his term, Hanson welcomed George Washington back to Philadelphia following his victory at Yorktown. Washington presented Cornwallis's sword to Congress. He also lightened his administrative burden by creating executive departments to deal with the myriad of correspondence and contracts, including the Treasury Department, the first Secretary of War, and the first Foreign Affairs Department. He saw to the removal of all foreign troops from American lands, as well as their flags. He gained agreement on the eventual statehood of the Western Territories. Hanson was also responsible for establishing Thanksgiving Day as the fourth Thursday in November. Elias Boudinot succeeded Hanson on November 5, 1782, but he continued as a delegate in the Congress for one more term.

In 1783, Hanson retired from Congress and returned to his nephew's estate near Oxon Hill in Prince George's County, Maryland. Oddly, word circulated in the papers that he had died in May 1783, but he had not. Retractions followed,

> The account published in the Philadelphia papers, of the death of the Honorable John Hanson, Esq; late President of Congress, we have the pleasure of assuring the public is premature; that worthy patriot being now in perfect health.

However, Hanson did die later in the year, on November 22, 1783. He was entombed on the estate at Oxon Hill, now known as the Addison Burial Ground. Unfortunately, the exact location of his grave has been lost, and the precise location of his remains is unknown. There was substantial development in the area, and the grave may have been vandalized.

According to biographer Seymour Weyss Smith, the American Revolution had two primary leaders: George Washington over the military and John Hanson in politics. However, this biography has been criticized as lacking academic support.

Of Hanson's children, Jane Contee Hanson (1747–1781) married Philip Thomas (1747–1815); Peter Contee Hanson, as mentioned, died at Fort Washington; and Alexander Contee Hanson (1749–1806) was a notable essayist. Alexander's son, by the same name, was a newspaper editor and U.S. senator from Maryland from 1813 to 1819.

John Hanson is one of the two Marylanders honored with a statue in the National Statuary Hall Collection in Washington, D.C. However, some lawmakers have recently lobbied to replace it with Harriet Tubman.

In 1972, Hanson was honored with a U.S. postal card featuring his name and portrait. He was also featured on a postage stamp. Route 50 between Washington, D.C., and Annapolis is named the John Hanson Highway. Middle schools in Oxon Hill and Waldorf, Maryland, are named after him. At one time, there was a bank named in his honor.

Since the 1970s, April 14 is John Hanson Day in Maryland thanks to a measure sponsored by descendent John Hanson Briscoe, who served as Speaker of the Maryland House of Delegates. The Hanson Memorial Association was created in 2009 to erect the John Hanson National Memorial and educate the public about Hanson. The memorial includes a statue at the courthouse in Frederick, Maryland.

Daniel of St. Thomas Jenifer
(1723–1790)

Elder Statesman

Probably buried at "Ellerslie" plantation family plot,
Port Tobacco, Maryland.

U.S. Constitution

Daniel of St. Thomas Jenifer was a plantation owner and Maryland politician who participated in the Continental Congress and signed the United States Constitution.

He was the son of Dr. Daniel Jenifer and Elizabeth Mason of Charles County, Maryland, near the town of Port Tobacco. The Jenifers' estate was then known as "Coates Retirement" (or "Retreat") and later "Ellerslie." The elder Jenifer was of English and Swedish ancestry. The reason for the linkage to St. Thomas is unclear. Some have surmised there was a family connection to either St. Thomas in the Virgin Islands or to the Parish of St. Thomas in County Cornwall, England.

Daniel was a popular name in the Jenifer family. The Founding Father's great-grandfather was Captain Daniel Jenifer (1637–1692/3) of Accomack County, Virginia, who later moved to Maryland. His son was Daniel of St. Thomas Jenifer (1672–1730). Then came Dr. Daniel (1699-1729) who had two sons, the Founder with the St. Thomas middle name, and another named (just) Daniel (1727–1795). That Daniel, the

MARYLAND PATRIOTS

Oil on canvas portrait of Daniel of St. Thomas Jenifer by John Hesselius.

brother of the Founder, had two sons; one named Daniel of St. Thomas Jenifer who died unmarried and one named Dr. Daniel Jenifer (1756–1809). This nephew subsequently had sons named Daniel of St. Thomas Jenifer (1789–1822) and Colonel Daniel Jenifer (1791–1855), who was a congressman and ambassador. This Daniel carried on the tradition of two sons; one named Daniel and another named Daniel of St. Thomas (1814-1843). Daniel of St. Thomas Jenifer, the Founder, was also the uncle of fellow Founder Thomas Stone as well as Michael Jenifer Stone and John Hoskins Stone.

Little is known about Daniel's childhood and education. Into young adulthood, he lived on and managed the estate near Port Tobacco before moving to Annapolis. Later in life, he lived at a plantation called

Daniel of St. Thomas Jenifer (1723–1790)

"Stepney" near Annapolis. Throughout his life, Jenifer was a substantial landowner and traded in slaves and indentured servants. He also had stakes in several local industries.

During the colonial period, prior to the Revolution, Jenifer acted as receiver-general for absentee proprietors in Maryland, collecting taxes and rents. He was well-liked and trusted by the locals, rising to justice of the peace and serving in many capacities including as a trusted advisor of the last royal governor of Maryland, Sir Robert Eden.

In 1760, Jenifer served on a boundary commission that helped settle the border disputes between Maryland, Pennsylvania, Delaware, and Virginia. Two English surveyors, Mason and Dixon, were hired from England to survey the boundaries.

As tensions mounted between the colonies and England, Jenifer put his economic might behind the patriot cause. He became the president of Maryland's Council of Safety that helped establish and organize the state militia. Later, he was president of the first state senate (1777–80), sat in the Continental Congress (1778–82), and held the position of Maryland state revenue and financial manager (1782–85). In his roles, Jenifer mostly served as a land manager, tracking and disposing of loyalist properties seized by patriots. He also used his deft financial management skills to help the state survive the postwar economic depression. Along with his friends George Washington, James Madison, George Mason, and John Dickinson, Jenifer worked collectively on solving the new nation's financial issues. To that end, he attended the Mount Vernon Conference, a precursor to the Constitutional Convention.

Jenifer was not the first choice to represent Maryland at the Constitutional Convention in Philadelphia, but when one of the four candidates backed out, he was asked to fill in. Upon his arrival, Jenifer was one of the elder statesmen present, younger only than his good friend Benjamin Franklin and Roger Sherman.

Despite his advancing years and physical limitations, Jenifer was one of only 29 delegates (of 55) who attended nearly every session. While he did not speak much, he used his good nature and humor to influence his colleagues and encourage compromise.

"Ellerslie" near Port Tobacco where the body of Daniel of St. Thomas Jenifer is buried somewhere on the grounds.

Philosophically, despite representing a small state, Jenifer was for Madison's Virginia Plan which espoused a strong central government with taxing authority. This put him at odds with fellow Marylander Luther Martin and given the regular absence of the two other delegates from the state, left them deadlocked. However, regarding the composition of the Senate, Martin was for equal representation among the states, as were the other smaller states. Out of courtesy, though he disagreed, the elderly Jenifer ambled out of Carpenter's Hall that July afternoon to allow Martin to vote on behalf of Maryland. He then returned to sign the Constitution, though Martin did not affix his signature.

Said Martin, "If the people support the Constitution, I will be hanged."

Jenifer quipped, "You should stay in Philadelphia so they don't get you with their ropes!"

After the convention, Jenifer returned to "Stepney" and lived out his remaining years, passing away in 1790. Daniel never married. He left most of his massive 10,000+ acre estate to his nephew Daniel Jenifer. He requested his slaves be freed six years after his death. He also bequeathed all his French-language books in his library to his good friend James Madison.

The exact location of Daniel of St. Thomas Jenifer's grave is unknown. Some suggest he was buried at "Stepney," while most believe he is buried in an unmarked grave at "Ellerslie" near Port Tobacco.

Jenifer Streets in Madison, Wisconsin and Washington, D.C. are named in his honor.

Thomas Johnson
(1732–1819)

One of the Original Supremes

Buried at Mount Olivet Cemetery,
Frederick, Maryland.

Continental Association • Continental Congress
Military • Supreme Court Justice

This founder served the young country in multiple positions during both the Revolutionary and post Constitution periods. He was elected to Maryland's colonial General Assembly, a position he held for more than a decade. He was a member of a committee established to study the constitutional rights of colonial Maryland citizens and to offer guidance to the Stamp Act Congress. He was one of the patriots who openly advocated a break with England when many of his contemporaries were urging a policy of reconciliation. He was a member of Maryland's Committee of Correspondence established to maintain communication with the other American colonies. He was elected to represent Maryland in the First Continental Congress. During the Revolution, he served as a brigadier general in the Maryland militia. He then was selected to be Maryland's first governor. After the Constitution's ratification, he became Chief Justice of the General Court of Maryland and then was appointed to be one of the first associate justices on the United States Supreme Court. The name of this accomplished American was Thomas Johnson.

Thomas Johnson (1732–1819)

Thomas Johnson

On November 4, 1731, Johnson was born near Saint Leonard's Creek in Calvert County, Maryland. He was the fifth of twelve children born to his father Thomas Johnson and his wife, Dorcas Johnson. When he was a boy, his parents moved the family to Annapolis. He received his education at home, and after studying the law, he was admitted to the colonial bar. He was working in the colonial land office where he met Anne Jennings, his boss's daughter. In 1766 Johnson married Jennings, and the couple would have seven children.

Johnson's initial foray into the political world came in 1762 when he was elected to the lower house of Maryland's Colonial Assembly. He served in that office until 1774. During this period, he also practiced law and invested in an iron furnace with three of his brothers near Frederick, Maryland.

MARYLAND PATRIOTS

Midway through 1774, a general meeting of representatives from all the colonies was called for with the delegates to meet in Philadelphia that September. Johnson was among the delegates selected to represent Maryland at what became known as the First Continental Congress. On October 20, 1774, Congress established the Continental Association, the colonial answer to the Coercive Acts passed by the British Parliament. These measures aimed to restructure the colonial administration in the American colonies and punish Massachusetts for the Boston Tea Party. The association imposed an immediate ban on British tea and, beginning December 1, 1774, banned importing or consuming any goods from England. Johnson favored these measures and was among the founders who signed the document creating the association.

A year later, Johnson affixed his signature on The Olive Branch Petition. In the petition, Congress made a plea to the British king to address the growing rifts between the mother country and the colonies. By this time, Congress was clearly unaware that the king had already made up his mind relative to the American colonies declaring that "the die is now cast" and that the colonists "must either submit or triumph." On June 15, 1775, as relations with England worsened, Johnson nominated George Washington to be the commander in chief of the Continental Army.

Having served in Congress with Johnson, John Adams offered his opinion that "Johnson, of Maryland, has a clear and cool head, an extensive knowledge of trade as well as the law. He is a deliberating man, but not a shining orator; his passion and imagination do not appear enough for an orator; his reason and penetration appear but not his rhetoric." There can be little doubt that Johnson was a deliberate man or viewed that as a strength. As he once told Adams, "We ought not to lay down a rule in passion."

In January of 1776, Johnson left Congress to serve as a brigadier general in the Maryland Colonial militia. During the winter months at the end of that year, Johnson led his troops to New Jersey to assist Washington during his retreat through that state.

The initial State Constitution of Maryland called for an election of a Governor by the two branches of the state legislature. That vote was taken in February of 1777, and Johnson was elected. He received forty votes compared to nine for Samuel Chase, who was the closest competitor.

Johnson was inaugurated as the state's first governor on March 21, 1777. When in the summer of that year, a British fleet under Admiral Howe's command sailed up the Chesapeake, Johnson issued a proclamation. In it, he called upon the people of his state to repel any possible invasion of Maryland. He noted that "Our wives, our children, and our country implore our assistance: motives amply sufficient to arm every man who can be called a man." The British fleet, for some reason, headed to Pennsylvania and invaded that state instead.

After his term as governor in 1779, Johnson moved to Frederick County, Maryland. A year later, he was elected to the Maryland House of Delegates. The first of three elections that would send him to serve in that body. In 1788 he was a delegate to the Maryland convention called to ratify the United States Constitution. A year later, President Washington appointed him to be the first United States Judge for the District of Maryland, but Johnson declined the appointment. In 1790 he did accept the post of the chief judge of the general court of Maryland. Then, in 1791, Washington chose him to be one of the first associate judges to serve on the United States Supreme Court.

The historian Timothy Hall wrote of Johnson's service on the highest court in the land: "Perhaps no justice ever came to a seat on the US Supreme Court more reluctantly than Maryland's Thomas Johnson, and no justice ever served on the Court for a shorter tenure than he did. By the last decade of the 18th century, age and bodily infirmity persuaded Johnson to retire from what had been a busy public life. But at the request of President George Washington, a longtime acquaintance and business partner, Johnson attempted the post of associate justice, only to discover shortly that 'the office and the man do not fit.' He left his seat on the court for a long retirement leaving little record of his brief presence there."

In August of 1795, following the resignation of Secretary of State Edmund Jennings Randolph, Washington offered the post to Johnson. Writing to his old friend, the president stated, "You know of my wishes of old to bring you into the administration. Where then is the necessity of my repeating them? No time more than the present ever required the aid of your abilities. To have yours would be pleasing to me, and I verily believe would be agreeable to the community at large. It is with you to

Thomas Johnson's grave.

decide." Johnson responded by pointing to his age and his health, saying, "I do not think that I could do credit to the office of Secretary. I cannot persuade myself that I possess the necessary qualifications for it, and I am sure I am too old to expect improvement."

Johnson's final public act was his memorial eulogy following Washington's death in 1799. Johnson passed away on October 25, 1819, at the Maryland estate of his son-in-law. He was laid to rest in the Johnson family vault in the All Saints Parish Cemetery in Frederick, Maryland. In 1913 his remains were moved to Mount Olivet Cemetery, also located in Frederick.

In considering Johnson's contributions to the country's founding, we should consider the words written by Richard Henry Lee's grandson. He called Johnson "one of the ablest men in the old Congress. There did not live in these times which 'tried men's souls' a purer patriot or a more efficient citizen. No Roman citizen ever loved his country more. His private virtues entitled him to veneration and love. Thomas Johnson was, indeed, an honor to the cause of liberty."

John Paul Jones
(1747–1792)

"I have not yet begun to fight!"

Buried at US Naval Academy Chapel,
Annapolis, Maryland.

Military

John Paul Jones, along with John Barry, John Adams, and others, is credited with being the "Father of the American Navy." Of Scottish descent, he served on British merchant ships before joining the Continental Navy during the American Revolution. There, he became the most famous naval hero during that conflict. However, after the war, he lost his command in the United States. He then served in the Russian Navy and died in Paris, France. His body was lost for over 100 years before it was rediscovered and ceremoniously returned to the United States in the early twentieth century.

John Paul was born on July 6, 1747, on the estate of Arbigland near Kirkbean in the Stewartry of Kirkcudbright, Scotland, to John Paul Sr., a gardener at the estate, and his wife, Jean McDuff. Kirkcudbright is in the southwest corner of Scotland, on the Irish Sea. The Estate of Arbigland was situated along the coast, owned by William Craik.

At age twelve or thirteen, circa 1760, Paul went to sea as a cabin boy on merchant marine and slave ships, including *King George* and *Two Friends*, plying the Atlantic slave trade between England, America, the West Indies, and Africa. His older brother, William Paul, had married and settled in Fredericksburg, Virginia, and John would visit when he

John Paul Jones

was on that side of the Atlantic. In Jamaica, in 1768, he left *Two Friends* and found passage back to Scotland.

In 1768, aboard the brig *John*, both the captain and first mate died of yellow fever. Paul took control and navigated the ship back to port. The grateful Scottish owners made him master of the ship and crew and gave him ten percent of the cargo. Now a captain, Paul led two voyages before running into trouble.

On the second voyage, 1770, Paul was accused of being unnecessarily cruel when he had a crewman flogged for trying to start a mutiny over wages. Though the claim was dismissed, his reputation was tarnished when the sailor, related to an influential family, died a few weeks later.

Paul was arrested and imprisoned at Kirkcudbright but was released on bail and encouraged to leave the area.

Now the commander of the 22-gun London-registered *Betsy*, John Paul headed out to sea. For nearly two years, he was engaged in trade with Tobago in the West Indies. Once again, Paul got in trouble with his crew. Some crewmen threatened a mutiny and attacked their captain. One of them, a man named Blackton, was killed in a swordfight with Paul. Fearing trouble with the Admiralty Court, Paul left Tobago and headed to Virginia, essentially a fugitive from justice.

In Fredericksburg, he found his brother had died without any immediate family, and he arranged his affairs. He then concealed his identity by appending the last name "Jones" and decided to stay in the colonies.

Now John Paul Jones, as the American Revolution commenced in late 1775, he joined the new Continental Navy as a lieutenant on the 24-gun flagship *Alfred*, thanks to an endorsement from Richard Henry Lee. On this voyage, he was the first to hoist the Grand Union Flag over a naval vessel. The *Alfred* raided military supplies in the Bahamas.

Jones was short in stature, possibly five feet five inches, earning him the nickname "Little Jones" with Thomas Jefferson and others. Unlike many other merchant seamen, he was well-dressed, wore a sword, and behaved nobly. He had a Scottish brogue, and light Celtic features. Though sociable, he was known as a harsh military master. A romantic who wrote poetry and letters and spoke French, he never married. However, he was involved in many romances. Above all, he was fearless.

By May 1776, he was made captain of the 21-gun sloop *Providence*, with which he destroyed British fisheries in Nova Scotia and captured sixteen British ships through the summer. Commodore Esek Hopkins then switched Jones back to captain the *Alfred*. He was ordered to rescue prisoners from Nova Scotia and to raid British shipping. That winter, he captured the *Mellish*, which was carrying winter clothing to General Burgoyne in Canada.

Due to disagreements with Commodore Hopkins about campaign plans, Jones was demoted to a smaller ship, the USS *Ranger*, on June 14, 1777. He sailed to France on November 1, 1777, to aid the American mission there. In France, he advised Benjamin Franklin, Silas Deane, and Arthur Lee regarding naval recommendations. He was promised command of a new vessel, *Indien*, which was being constructed in Amsterdam. However, the British managed to pressure the Dutch to sell it to France, leaving Jones without a command. During this time, he developed a close friendship with Franklin.

After France agreed to enter the war on the Americans' side in February 1778, Jones was back at sea about USS *Ranger*. His was the first American vessel to be formally saluted by the French. In April, he set sail for the familiar Irish Sea, between Ireland and England, and harassed British shipping.

On April 17, 1778, he convinced his crew to attack Whitehaven, England, where he had begun his maritime career. However, the winds drove them toward Ireland. There, they attempted to attack HMS *Drake* anchored at Carrickfergus, Ireland. The sailors balked at attacking in broad daylight, and the night attack was botched by the mate who was to drop anchor when they were next to their target. So, Jones turned *Ranger* out to sea and headed back to Whitehaven. On the night of the 23rd, Jones and two boats of fifteen men attempted to set fire to and sink all of Whitehaven's ships, including merchant and coal transports. While they were able to spike the defensive cannons, they had difficulty starting enough fires. They were forced to retreat when the townspeople were alerted.

Next, crossing to Scotland, he headed to St. Mary's Isle near Kirkcudbright to attempt to capture Dunbar Douglas, the Earl of Selkirk. They found the earl missing and instead negotiated with his wife. The butler handed Jones a bag of coal with some silver on top, fooling the Americans that they had a bag of treasure. The crew had wanted to continue plundering, but Jones wanted to return to the ship. He permitted them to only take a large silver tray with the Selkirk coat of arms, which he later bought at auction and returned to the earl after the war.

Jones then turned *Ranger* back to Carrickfergus to engage the *Drake* again. On the afternoon of April 24, 1778, the two ships battled until the British captain was slain. The Americans captured the *Drake,* and Jones put his lieutenant, Simpson, in charge of it. While returning to

John Paul Jones (1747–1792)

Brest, France, the two ships separated due to Jones chasing another prize. Though both ships reached port safely, Jones filed for court-martial against Simpson for unclear reasons and detained him on the ship. Simpson was ultimately released, however.

Jones was promoted and placed in command of five French and American vessels in 1779. His flagship was now the 42-gun USS *Bonhomme Richard*, named in honor of Benjamin Franklin's character Poor Richard. In August, Jones's squadron set sail for the Irish Sea, acting as a diversion for a large Spanish and French fleet heading to England. British ships pursued Jones as he broke away and sailed around Scotland into the North Sea. While closing on a merchant convoy, The *Bonhomme Richard* encountered the 50-gun HMS *Serapis* and the 22-gun *Countess of Scarborough*. As the merchant ships escaped, what was known as the Battle of Flamborough Head began. While *Serapis* engaged *Bonhomme Richard*, the American ship *Alliance* fired at *Countess*. Jones brought *Bonhomme* close to *Serapis*. The ships and crews fired at one another, clearing the decks. The *Alliance* then sailed past, firing a broadside that damaged both ships. *Countess* was pulled away to engage one of the other American ships downwind.

Bonhomme Richard was now burning and sinking. *Serapis* came alongside and, seeing the ensign shot away, asked if the *Bonhomme* would surrender. Believing Jones dead, one of the American officers shouted a surrender, but Jones appeared and shouted something like, "I am determined to make you strike." Some heard him say, "I may sink, but I'll be damned if I strike." But he never actually said, "I have not yet begun to fight!"

Things got uglier. The *Serapis*' crew tried to board the *Bonhomme* but were repulsed when a grenade ignited gunpowder on the lower decks of the British attacker. The *Alliance* came around again and blasted both ships. Captain Pearson of the *Serapis*, seeing no chance to escape, struck his colors and surrendered. Most of the crew of the *Bonhomme Richard* then transferred to the British ship. Jones took command. After trying to repair the *Bonhomme Richard* over the next two days proved fruitless, the ship was allowed to sink and Jones and his squadron headed for Texel, Holland.

The following year, while the British saw Jones as a pirate, French King Louis XVI granted him the title Chevalier. He also received a sword and *l'Institution du Mérite Militaire* (Order of Military Merit). With the Revolutionary War nearing its end, Jones was to take command of the new 74-gun USS *America* in June 1782. However, the ship was traded to the French as a replacement for the *Le Magnifique*, which had been lost off Boston that year. Jones was next assigned to collect the prize money due his former crew from the ships captured and left in European ports.

In 1787, when the Continental Congress struck a gold medal honoring him for his "valor and brilliant service," Jones made sure the title Chevalier was used. However, he was without prospects, and on April 23, 1787, entered the service of Empress Catherine II of Russia as a rear admiral aboard the 24-gun flagship *Vladimir*. He participated in the Liman campaign against the Turks in the Black Sea. While victorious, Jones transferred to the North Sea due to other officers' jealousy, some British also serving Russia. Jones was accused of sexual misconduct, allegedly raping a 12-year-old girl, but a French emissary investigated on his behalf and found the charges baseless. Jones admitted to "frolicking with the girl for a small cash payment" but denied he had taken her virginity. During this time, he authored the *Narrative of the Campaign of the Liman*.

On June 8, 1788, the Russians awarded him the Order of St. Anne. Jones next went to Warsaw, Poland, in 1789, where he linked up with Tadeusz Kościuszko, the Polish general who served in the American Revolution. Kościuszko suggested Jones should leave the service of Russia and seek opportunities in Sweden. This, however, never materialized.

Though retaining his position as a rear admiral for Russia, Jones moved to Paris in May 1790. He benefitted from a pension for his service, and he tried numerous times to return to active duty. All were rebuffed.

Jones wrote his memoirs and had them published in Edinburgh. He planned to purchase an estate in the United States and had been appointed the US Consul to Algiers, but neither came to fruition due to his declining health. Jones was found dead lying face-down on his bed in his third-floor Paris apartment, No. 19 Rue de Tournon, on July 18, 1792. He was 45 years old. The cause of death was kidney disease. Frenchman

John Paul Jones (1747-1792)

Pierrot Francois Simmoneau funded the mummification of the body and saw it was preserved in alcohol and interred in a lead coffin "in the event that should the United States decide to claim his remains, they might more easily be identified." Jones was buried at Saint Louis Cemetery in Paris, which belonged to the royal family. After the French Revolution, the property was sold, and the cemetery was forgotten.

Over the ensuing years, Jones appeared in the novel *The Pilot* in 1824 by James Fenimore Cooper. Alexander Dumas followed with *Captain Paul* in 1846. Jones also made a cameo in Herman Melville's novel *Israel Potter: His Fifty Years of Exile*. He appealed to historians and novelists due to his personality ad his accomplishments against the most powerful navy in the world.

The gaudy tomb of John Paul Jones at the US Naval Academy.

US Ambassador to France General Horace Porter, circa 1900, began a six-year search to locate Jones's remains. Using an old Paris map, Porter and his team found the cemetery and located and exhumed five lead coffins. The third coffin, unearthed on April 7, 1905, later proved to contain Jones. The cause of death was analyzed, and his face compared to a bust by Jean-Antoine Houdon.

With great decorum, Jones's body was returned to the United States aboard the USS *Brooklyn*, escorted by three other cruisers. As the ships neared the coast, nine other battleships joined the procession. The following year, the remains were installed at the US Naval Academy in Bancroft Hall. President Theodore Roosevelt presided over a ceremony to honor Jones. In 1913, his remains were interred into a bronze and marble sarcophagus in the Naval Academy Chapel.

Jones has since appeared in many movies, books, and television programs. In 1999, the Port of Whitehaven pardoned him for the raid.

According to biographer Walter Herrick, "Jones was a sailor of indomitable courage, of strong will, and of great ability in his chosen career . . . He was also a hypocrite, a brawler, a rake, and a professional and social climber."

To many, he is also the founder of the United States Navy and emblematic of American courage.

Edward Langworthy
(1738–1802)

An Orphaned Founder

He was initially buried at the Old Episcopal Church in Baltimore, Maryland. The church was demolished in 1891, and the location of his remains is unknown.

Articles of Confederation

This founder's parents were likely among the first colonists shipped to Georgia. This conclusion is because he was born within five years of James Oglethorpe recruiting those in poorhouses and debtors' prisons to be the first to settle in the region. It appears his parents died when he was very young as he was raised in the Bethesda Orphan House in Savannah. Despite these challenging beginnings, he would rise to represent Georgia in the Continental Congress during the American Revolution and sign the Articles of Confederation. This document officially united the thirteen colonies as a country. Described by Burton Alva Knokle in *The Georgia Historical Quarterly* as a patriot, teacher, statesman, editor, writer, historian, and eminent citizen of two states, this founder's name was Edward Langworthy.

Langworthy was born in Savannah circa 1738. It appears his parents died when he was relatively young as he was raised and educated in Savannah's Bethesda Orphan House. He took his studies seriously as he became one of the instructors at the orphanage. At one point, he took out an advertisement in a Georgia newspaper which read, "The subscriber having taken a convenient House, proposes to board eight young gentlemen at 22 per annum, and to instruct them in the Latin and Greek Languages. The greatest care will be taken to improve them in the English language and to accustom them to a just and agreeable manner in pronunciation and reading. Young ladies may be taught English Grammar, Writing, &c. privately." It appears that teaching as a profession appealed to him since he would take up the profession again later in life.

Edward Langworthy

In 1774, when the fires that became the American Revolution were already burning, Langworthy remained loyal to the British crown, as evidenced by his signing the Loyalist protest of the Savannah Resolutions. His Loyalist leanings did not last long as, within a year, he reversed his position entirely and was chosen secretary to the Revolutionary body known as the Council of Safety. Two months later, he became a member of the Georgia Provincial Congress, where he was appointed secretary of that body. In this position, Langworthy signed the initial delegates' credentials to represent Georgia at the Continental Congress meeting in Philadelphia. Among the credentials he signed was one for a good friend of his, Button Gwinnett. Gwinnett would affix his signature to the Declaration of Independence.

On June 7, 1777, the Georgia legislature elected Langworthy to serve as a delegate to the Continental Congress. As a representative from Georgia, he signed the Articles of Confederation on July 24, 1778. The Articles formally brought the thirteen states together, forming the United States of America. He was not a vocal member of Congress as he is not recorded as ever having made a motion though he did second on two occasions. He was among the representatives who spent time in York, Pennsylvania, when the Congress was moved there after the British army occupied Philadelphia. Based on a letter he wrote at the time, he had little liking for the city. After completing his service in Congress, Langworthy returned to Georgia, where he may well have begun the research on the state's first history, which he would work on for years but never complete. His papers involving this project have never been recovered.

In 1785, Langworthy moved to Baltimore, where he became part owner and the editor of the *Maryland Journal & Baltimore Advertiser*. The newspaper flourished and proved to be a successful business venture. In one open letter to the paper's readers, Langworthy and his co-owner, William Goddard, stated, "It would perhaps be to little Purpose to descant on the many Advantages derived from the Art of Printing; that the present Age is esteemed an Enlightened One, and that we are in the enjoyment of Political Independence, and Perfect Freedom in the important Concerns of Religion, may, in a great Degree, be ascribed to the Liberty of the Press."

When Langworthy was busy with his newspaper, the Baltimore religious heads of the Catholic, Episcopalian, and Presbyterian churches established the Baltimore Academy. The institution's purpose was to provide the young men in the area an opportunity to pursue a higher education without leaving home. Langworthy was chosen to head the school where he also taught the classics. It is not clear how long he labored at the Academy. It is known that he sold his interest in the newspaper on January 1, 1787, and that in March of that year, he completed his memoir of General Charles Lee. In 1792 this work was published in both New York and London.

In 1795, Langworthy was appointed to the post of Baltimore's Clerk of Customs. He would serve in this position until he died on November 2, 1802. He had impressed many in the Baltimore area relative to his conduct and life in his adopted second city.

His obituary stated, "After a severe illness of six days . . . the spirit of Edward Langworthy, Esq. deputy naval officer of the port of Baltimore, took its flight for 'another and a better world.' To eulogize the defunct is not the intention of the writer of this paragraph, suffice it to say, that his public and private walks in life were such as many may endeavor to imitate, but a few will attain to equal perfection."

Langworthy was laid to rest in the yard of Baltimore's Old Episcopal Church. That church was demolished in 1891, and the records of the graveyard were lost.

Thomas Lynch
(1727–1776)
South Carolina Son of Liberty

Buried at Saint Anne's Churchyard,
Annapolis, Maryland

Continental Association

Thomas Lynch, Sr., was a South Carolina planter who served in the Stamp Act Congress and Continental Congress, where he signed the Continental Association. Before signing the Declaration of Independence, he was stricken, and his son, Thomas Lynch, Jr., took his place.

Thomas Lynch was born circa 1727, in St. James Santee Parish, Berkeley County, South Carolina, the son of Thomas Lynch, a wealthy rice planter, and his wife, Sabina (née Vanderhorst) Lynch. This elder Lynch was likely the grandson of Jonack Lynch, who emigrated from Connaught Ireland, in the late 1600s. He had decided to forego planting silkworms and Indian corn instead planting rice and indigo. He had grants for fifteen thousand acres in Craven County, on the North and South Santee Rivers, between Charles Towne and Georgetown. By the time he died in 1738, he had amassed seven plantations and nearly two hundred slaves.

As the only surviving child, Lynch inherited his family's vast estates. Lynch first married Elizabeth Allston in 1745 and fathered three children. He married second Hannah Motte, the daughter of Jacob Motte

Thomas Lynch (1727–1776)

Thomas Lynch

and Elizabeth Martin, on March 6, 1755. This marriage produced a daughter and Thomas Lynch, Jr. Hannah's brother, Isaac Motte, was later a South Carolina Congressman. Following Hannah's death during childbirth, Lynch married Annabella Josephiné Dé'Illiard.

Lynch served as a representative for the Parish of St. James, Santee, in the House of Commons and Provincial Assembly from 1751 to 1757, 1761 to 1763, 1765, 1768, and 1772. He was the first president of the Winyah Indigo Society from 1755 to 1757 and was the second wealthiest person in the colony.

Upon passage of the Stamp Act in Parliament, Lynch was a delegate to the Stamp Act Congress of 1765 in New York. He served on a committee that drafted a petition to the House of Commons demanding the Act be repealed. In 1769, Lynch served on the General Committee of the Non-Importation Association. He then helped run the colony in the years leading up to the Revolution while colonial governor Charles Montagu was absent.

Visiting Charleston in early 1773, the Massachusetts lawyer and patriot Josiah Quincy described Lynch as "a man of sense, and a patriot." Lynch was highly active with the Sons of Liberty in South Carolina. In July of 1774, Lynch, Henry Middleton, John Rutledge, Christopher Gadsden, and Edward Rutledge were sent to the Continental Congress to represent South Carolina in Philadelphia that September. Wrote Silas Deane to his wife about Lynch,

> I will now give you the character of the Delegates, beginning at South Carolina, as they are the Southernmost. Mr. Lynch is a gentleman about sixty, and could you see him; I need say nothing more. He has much the appearance of Mr. Ja[mes] Mumford, deceased; dresses as plain, or plainer; is of immense fortune, and has his family with him. He wears the manufacture of this country, is plain, sensible, above ceremony, and carries with him more fore in his very appearance than most powdered folks in their conversation. He wears his hair strait [sic], his clothes in the plainest order, and is highly esteemed.

Lynch was an active member of the First Continental Congress, earning the respect of his fellow delegates. While he returned home to South Carolina in October 1774 after signing the Continental Association, he was re-elected to the Congress on March 4, 1775, along with the same group.

The following month, shots were fired at Lexington and Concord. Lynch was a supporter of appointing George Washington as the Commander-in-Chief of the Continental Army. He was able, through John Adams, to convince the New England delegation and then convinced the Southern delegation. Congress then appointed Washington.

Lynch joined Benjamin Franklin and Benjamin Harrison on a committee sent to Cambridge, Massachusetts, to discuss with General George

Washington about "the most effectual method of continuing, supporting, and regulating the Continental Army." Washington mentioned his plan to arm ships to raid the British supply lines. The committee liked the idea and recommended it to Congress, thereby establishing "George Washington's Navy," the nation's first organized naval force.

Back home, Lynch was elected by St. James Santee Parish to the Second Provincial Congress for 1775 to 1776 and the first South Carolina General Assembly for 1776 but did not participate. Lynch was back in Philadelphia in 1776 as a member of the Second Continental Congress. He participated in the discussions concerning independence but suffered a debilitating stroke, paralyzing him. Thomas Lynch, Jr., was dispatched to Congress as an additional delegate to assist his father at the signing of the Declaration of Independence. The fifty-five other delegates left a blank space between Heywood and Rutledge in the South Carolina section of the document in honor of the elder Lynch.

After the document was signed, the Lynches headed back to South Carolina, but Lynch suffered another stroke and died on the way in December 1776. An obituary from the time stated,

> From the announcement of the present struggle in favour of American freedom, this gentleman acted a distinguished part and proved himself the firm, intrepid patriot. In private life, he was not less conspicuous, a warm and steady friend, hospitable, generous, and benevolent. He died in the fiftieth year of his age, greatly regretted by his relations and countrymen.

Rather than transporting his father's body hundreds of miles, Lynch Jr. buried him in St. Anne's Churchyard in Annapolis, Maryland. The younger Lynch followed in his father's footsteps in Congress until he was lost at sea in 1779.

After Lynch's death, his widow Annabella married South Carolina Governor William Moultrie. Lynch's daughter Elizabeth married James Hamilton. Their son, James Hamilton Jr., was elected governor of South Carolina in 1830 and led the state through the Nullification crisis through 1832.

James McHenry
(1753–1816)

Secretary of War

Buried at Westminster Hall and Burying Ground,
Baltimore, Maryland

U.S. Constitution

James McHenry was a military surgeon and statesman who signed the U.S. Constitution on behalf of Maryland. He was a member of the Continental Congress, secretary to General George Washington, aide-de-camp to Marquis de Lafayette, and secretary of war bridging the Washington and Adams administrations.

James McHenry was born November 16, 1753, in Ballymena, in County Antrim, Ireland, the son of Daniel McHenry, a merchant, and his wife, Agnes. The family was Scotch Irish Presbyterian.

McHenry was sent to Dublin as a boy to receive a classical education. However, he became ill while at school and was sent to America in 1771 to improve his health. McHenry was placed in the care of family friend Captain William Allison of Philadelphia. There, he met Allison's stepdaughter, Margaret Caldwell, whom he subsequently married. McHenry's parents and siblings joined him in Baltimore soon after. McHenry's father opened a merchant shop with his son John called McHenry and Son.

McHenry finished his preparatory education at Newark Academy, now the University of Delaware. He then returned to Philadelphia to

James McHenry (1753–1816)

James McHenry

study medicine as an apprentice to Benjamin Rush. McHenry became a physician.

When the Revolution broke out in 1775, McHenry traveled to Cambridge, Massachusetts, and met with George Washington to offer his medical services. In January 1776, he was assigned to the military hospital in Cambridge and was recognized for his skill by the Continental Congress. On August 10, McHenry was named the surgeon for Colonel Robert Magaw's 5th Pennsylvania Battalion, but he was captured at the fall of Fort Washington in November. McHenry was paroled on January 27, 1777, but remained in Philadelphia and Baltimore until a prisoner exchange was completed in March 1778.

Upon his return to service, McHenry was the senior surgeon at Valley Forge until May 15, 1778, when he was appointed the secretary to Washington. He held this position until 1780, when he was named

Lafayette's aide-de-camp. McHenry remained in this position until the end of the war.

Back in Maryland in 1781, McHenry was elected to the Maryland State Senate, where he served until 1786. He was elected by the Maryland General Assembly to the Continental Congress on May 12, 1783, serving through 1785. He was elected a member of the American Philosophical Society in January 1786.

In 1787, Maryland selected as delegates to the U.S. Constitutional Convention Daniel Carroll, Daniel of St. Thomas Jenifer, Luther Martin, John Francis Mercer, and James McHenry. At the convention held in Philadelphia in the summer of 1787, McHenry took copious notes on all matters debated before and by the delegates. His notations provide historians a moment-by-moment examination of how the U.S. Constitution came together. For instance, at the opening of the parley, he wrote:

> On the 25th [of May], seven states being represented viz. In New York, New Jersey, Pennsylvania, Delaware, Virginia, North Carolina, and South Carolina, George Washington was elected (unanimously) president of the convention. The convention appoint a committee to prepare and report rules for conducting business which were reported, debated, and in general agreed to on the 28th.
>
> 29 [May]. Governor Randolph opened the business of the convention. (2) He observed that the confederation fulfilled none of the objects for which it was framed. 1st. It does not provide against foreign invasions. 2dly. It does not secure harmony to the States. 3d. It is incapable of producing certain blessings to the States. 4. It cannot defend itself against encroachments. 5th. It is not superior to State constitutions.
>
> 1st. It does not provide against foreign invasion. If a State acts against a foreign power contrary to the laws of nations or violates a treaty, it cannot punish that State, or compel its obedience to the treaty. It can only leave the offending State to the operations of the

offended power. It, therefore, cannot prevent a war. If the rights of an ambassador be invaded by any citizen, it is only in a few States that any laws exist to punish the offender. A State may encroach on foreign possessions in its neighborhood, and Congress cannot prevent it. Disputes that respect naturalization cannot be adjusted. None of the judges in the several States under the obligation of an oath to support the confederation, in which view this writing will be made to yield to State constitutions.

McHenry missed much of the convention due to his brother's illness but was an active speaker when present. He signed the Constitution and then helped to see it ratified by Maryland. He returned to state politics in 1788 when he was elected to the Maryland House of Delegates on October 10. After two years in the role, he spent a year in the mercantile business before accepting a term in the Maryland Senate on November 15, 1791. He served five years.

In 1792, McHenry purchased a 95-acre tract from Ridgely's Delight near Baltimore and named it Fayetteville in honor of his friend, the Marquis de Lafayette.

During President Washington's second term, in 1796, McHenry was appointed secretary of war, a cabinet position overseeing the entire American military establishment, Indian affairs, and naval activity. His initial task was to transition Western military posts ceded from Great Britain under the terms of the Jay Treaty. Subsequently, McHenry's primary focus was to prepare for a possible war with either France or England.

When the Adams administration followed in 1797, McHenry continued in his role as secretary of war. However, he had a strained relationship with him. After a stormy cabinet meeting in May 1800, Adams requested McHenry's resignation. He resigned on May 13. In a letter to his friend Hugh Williamson, dated May 29, 1800, McHenry wrote of his being relieved of his services:

> I have not now time to communicate to you the particulars which [unintelligible] to the late changes in the Executive offices. Perhaps

Ft. Henry bombardment 1814

you will discover some of the causes in the man stabs evidently taken by the President to receive its diction. He has certainly acted and is daily acting in a manner to break up the federal party [sic] and destroy any remaining confidence many may have in him. He cannot hear Washington praised without intolerable pain and hates with inconceivable acrimony those who consider that great man to have outstripped him in virtuous and honorable reputation. It is certain that all of our courtesies to the opposition and measures to secure votes will not divert a single one from Jefferson.

During the election of 1800, McHenry urged Alexander Hamilton to release a pamphlet questioning Adams's loyalty and patriotism. This was controversial and paved the way for Thomas Jefferson to become president.

Now retired at his home, McHenry kept up his correspondence with his friends and associates. He frequently conversed with Timothy

Pickering and Benjamin Tallmadge about the Federalists and the War of 1812. In 1812, Fort McHenry was erected in Baltimore Harbor and named in his honor. He was also elected president of the Bible Society of Baltimore in 1813.

The grave of James McHenry

In 1814, McHenry was stricken by an attack of paralysis from which he was in severe pain and lost the use of his legs. On September 13, 1814, British naval vessels bombarded Fort McHenry during the War of 1812. This event was the basis for Francis Scott Key's "Star-Spangled Banner."

Despite his failing health, McHenry was elected a member of the American Antiquarian Society in July 1815. On May 3, 1816, he died at his estate and was buried in the Westminster Presbyterian Churchyard in Baltimore. His gravestone reads, "James McHenry. Signer of the Constitution." Upon the death of her beloved husband, Mrs. McHenry wrote:

> Here we come to the end of a life of a courteous, high-minded, keen-spirited, Christian gentleman. He was not a great man but participated in great events, and great men loved him, while all men appreciated his goodness and purity of soul. His highest titles to remembrance are that he was faithful to every duty and that he was the intimate and trusted friend of Lafayette, of Hamilton, and of Washington.

Biographer Karen Robbins wrote in 1994,

> James McHenry was a man of integrity and talent, with successes and failures, who served his country to the best of his ability, and whose story sheds light on the problems within the Federalist Party during the Adams administration. From an early point, this Scots-Irish immigrant emerged as a cautious man, slow to decide but steadfast once committed, who was transformed into a colonist, a patriot, a politician, and, finally, a Federalist.

James McHenry has been honored by Henry Street in Madison, Wisconsin, and the town of McHenry, Maryland, in Garrett County, was named after him. He was also memorialized at Independence Hall and the National Constitution Center in Philadelphia.

William Paca
(1740–1799)

Master of Wye

Buried at "Wye House" plantation,
Queenstown, Maryland.

Continental Association • Declaration of Independence

In his time he was viewed as a handsome, fashionable, and educated gentleman who was willing to risk his life and his property for the cause of American independence. Benjamin Rush said that he was "loved and respected by all" and at all times "a sincere patriot and honest man." He signed the Declaration of Independence as a Maryland representative to the Continental Congress. One of the reasons so little is known about the man is that all his papers and diaries were lost in a fire. Born on October 31, 1740, his name was William Paca.

Paca was the second son born to John Paca and his wife Elizabeth. The family also included five daughters. Paca's father was wealthy Maryland planter and the owner of a large estate. As a result, Paca had the good fortune of receiving an excellent and well-rounded education. First he attended the Philadelphia Academy and Charity School before moving on to the College of Philadelphia (now known as the University of Pennsylvania) where he graduated with a Bachelor of Arts degree in 1759. Three years later he received a Master of Arts degree from the same institution.

MARYLAND PATRIOTS

Portrait of William Paca by Charles Willson Peale, circa 1772

With his education complete, Paca returned to Maryland and settled in Annapolis where he studied law under Stephen Bordley who was widely considered to be the finest attorney in the colony at the time. During this period, he married Mary Chew the daughter of another prominent Maryland planter and in 1764 he was admitted to the Maryland provincial bar.

Two other future signers of the Declaration of Independence, Samuel Chase and Thomas Stone, were also living in Annapolis engaged in the study of law. The three young patriots became friends with Chase and Paca, in particular, earning less than stellar reputations as far as local officials loyal to the crown were concerned. On one occasion the duo decided to stage a mock execution of a law that had been recently enacted by the royal governor. After copying the law to a sheet of paper, they took it to a mock gallows where it was hanged until it was dead. They then cut it down and burned it in a coffin as a ship owned by Paca fired a cannon shot from the Chesapeake Bay to celebrate the moment. Paca and Chase were also instrumental in the formation of the Anne Arundel County chapter of the Sons of Liberty. It was through this organization that they organized and led the local opposition to the British Stamp Act of 1765.

Paca's biographers Gregory A. Stiverson and Phoebe R. Jacobsen maintain that despite these demonstrations, Paca was no mere rabble-rouser. They maintain that "Paca preferred fighting injustice and oppression by constructing finely argued newspaper essays that traced constitutional precedents and appealed to man's natural rights." This description seems in keeping with those who would work with him later in the Continental Congress and with the manner in which he led his own life.

Paca was elected to the Maryland legislature in 1771 and was appointed to represent the state as a member of the Continental Congress in 1774. With this honor and responsibility, the year also brought grief to Paca when his wife died after giving birth to their third child. He served in Congress until 1779 and during that five-year period was among those who voted in favor of American independence and signed the document proclaiming it. John Adams praised Paca relative to the debate on American independence describing him as a "deliberator" who performed "generously and nobly" during the discussions that led to the declaration.

In 1777, Paca remarried. His second wife Ann Harrison was the daughter of a wealthy and socially prominent Philadelphia merchant. This marriage was short-lived as Ann passed away in 1780 after a long illness.

Paca's contributions to the country and to Maryland did not end when he left the Continental Congress. He spent thousands of dollars supplying the troops from Maryland who fought in the Revolution. He served as Maryland's Chief Justice and as the state's Governor. During his term as Governor he worked to provide assistance to the veterans who had fought for and won America's independence. He strongly supported the Articles of Confederation and opposed the Constitution during the ratification fight on the grounds that the federal government it created was too powerful and that it contained no bill of rights. Some of his objections were used as foundations for the initial amendments to the Constitution.

Paca fathered two children out of wedlock. The mother of one of these children was a free black woman. Paca acknowledged that he was the child's father and sent her to the best schools available. This admirable conduct was said to raise more than a few eyebrows in the young country at the time.

In 1789 President Washington appointed Paca to the Federal District Court for Maryland. It was a post he held until his death at his estate on Wye Island on October 13, 1799. Paca was laid to rest on the grounds of his estate. The estate is on private property that is posted with signs to discourage trespassers. However, every July 4th there is a wreath-laying ceremony held at Paca's grave that is often attended by his descendants.

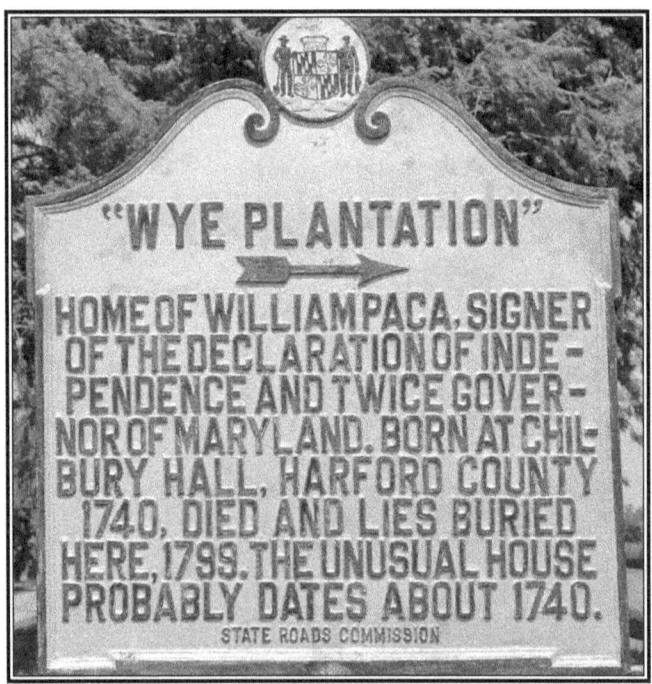

Historic marker about William Paca's "Wye House" plantation in Queen Anne County, Maryland, which is private property (photo by Lawrence Knorr).

Thomas Stone
(1743–1787)

Pacificist Patriot

*Buried at Thomas Stone National Historic Site,
Port Tobacco, Maryland.*

Declaration of Independence

Thomas Stone was a plantation owner and lawyer who represented Maryland in the Continental Congress and signed the Declaration of Independence. Later, he worked on the committee that created the Articles of Confederation and briefly acted as President of Congress in 1784.

Stone was born at "Poynton Manor" in Charles County, Maryland, the second son of David Stone and Elizabeth Jenifer Stone. He was the great great grandson of William Stone, the immigrant, who settled in Accomack County, Virginia, in 1628 and became a wealthy landowner and political leader including Governor of Maryland in 1648. In 1654 William moved the family to Maryland where he was given "Poynton Manor" for his services to Lord Baltimore. Thomas Stone's brothers, Michael J. Stone and John Hoskins Stone, also had important political careers. They were all the nephews of Daniel of St. Thomas Jenifer, through their mother.

Thomas grew up near the village of Welcome, Maryland, and was an ardent student. As a teenager, he rode ten miles on horseback to be

Portrait of Thomas Stone by Robert Edge Pine, 1785.

tutored in Latin and Greek by a Scottish schoolmaster named Blaizedel. He subsequently studied law with Thomas Johnson in Annapolis, Maryland, and was admitted to the bar in 1764, at the age of 21. He then started a law practice in Frederick, Maryland, and represented clients circuit riding from Frederick to Annapolis to Philadelphia. After a couple of years, he moved his law office back to Charles County.

At the age of 25, in 1768, Thomas married eighteen-year-old Margaret Brown, the daughter of Dr. Gustavus R. Brown and his second wife, Margaret Black Boyd. Stone received a dowry of one thousand pounds sterling with which he purchased a farm near the village of Port Tobacco, Maryland, which he named "Habre de Venture." Dr. Brown had a role in the founding of Charlestown at the head of the Port Tobacco Creek and built a home called "Rose Hill" which is on the National Register of Historic Places. His son, by the same name, followed in his father's footsteps and became a wealthy physician and close friend of George Washington. It was Dr. Gustavus Brown, Jr., the brother-in-law of Thomas Stone, who attended to the former President during his final illness at "Mount Vernon."

The young Stone family added three children: Margaret (1771-1809), Mildred (1773-1837), and Frederick (1774-1793). Upon the death of his father in 1773, the entire estate went to Thomas's older brother. This left Thomas with the increased responsibility of four younger brothers and two younger sisters in addition to his own three children. "Habre de Venture" was increased to accommodate the suddenly larger family.

To keep up with the expenses of his household, Stone continued his law practice and utilized his younger brother Michael to manage the plantation. At one point, Stone was involved in a lawsuit regarding a poll tax and the clergy and found himself on opposite sides from Samuel Chase and William Paca with whom he would later serve in the Continental Congress.

In 1774, Thomas joined the Charles County Committee of Correspondence, opposing British policies towards the colonies. From 1774 to 1776, he was a member of Maryland's Annapolis Convention, the body governing Maryland in the early days of the Revolution. In 1775, this convention sent Stone as a delegate to the Continental Congress where he and most of his fellow Marylanders initially favored reconciliation with Great Britain. He was a signer of the Olive Branch Petition that attempted to avoid hostilities. His views about the increasing tensions are expressed in this letter:

> I wish to conduct affairs so that a just and honorable reconciliation should take place, or that we should be pretty unanimous in a resolution to fight it out for independence. The proper way to effect this is not to move too quick. But then we must take care to do everything which is necessary for our security and defense, not suffer ourselves to be lulled or wheedled by any deceptions, declarations or givings out. You know my heart wishes for peace upon terms of security and justice to America. But war, anything, is preferable to a surrender of our rights.

MARYLAND PATRIOTS

Entering 1776, sentiment across the colonies moved towards independence. Stone wrote to his friend James Holyday,

> The die is cast. The fatal stab is given to any future connection between this country & Britain, except in the relation of conqueror & vanquished, which I can't think of without horror & indignation . . .

Stone was also moved towards independence despite the caution of many of his constituents. Representing Maryland, on May 15, 1776, he voted in favor of drafting a declaration of independence. This was soon followed by Richard Henry Lee's resolution for independence on June 7.

As the calendar turned to July, there was to be no peace settlement with England. The Maryland Convention had a change of heart and gave permission to the delegates to support independence. The vote was held July 4, 1776, with the Maryland delegation in the affirmative. Wrote Stone to the Maryland Council of Safety on July 12,

> May God send victory to the arm lifted in support of righteousness, virtue & freedom, and crush even to destruction the power which wantonly would trample on the rights of mankind.

Stone signed the Declaration of Independence on August 2, 1776.

Stone was elected a Maryland state senator in September and served in that capacity for several years. He also was assigned to the committee that drafted the Articles of Confederation but had to leave Philadelphia due to his wife taking ill after being vaccinated for smallpox, possibly due to the presence of mercury in the vaccine. Unfortunately, her health declined for the rest of her life, pulling Stone into seclusion as he cared for her.

Though elected to Congress in 1783, he retired after one term. He did remain active locally, practicing law in Annapolis, including participation in the Mount Vernon Convention in 1785. He was elected to the Constitutional Convention in 1787 but declined due to the deterioration of his wife's health. Margaret Stone finally succumbed to her long illness in 1787 at the age of thirty-six. Devastated, Thomas withdrew from public life.

Following her death, Stone was encouraged by his physicians to take a sea voyage. He began his preparations and headed to Annapolis. Before the vessel was to set sail, and only four months after Margaret's passing, on October 5, 1787, Thomas died of a "broken heart." He was only forty-four. He was buried in the family plot on his estate which is now managed by the National Park Service.

Said a fellow member in the Maryland state senate of Thomas Stone,

> . . . A talented writer. He was most truly a perfect man of business; he would often take the pen and commit to paper all the necessary writings of the Senate, and this he would do cheerfully while the other members were amusing themselves with desultory conversation; he appeared to be naturally of an irritable temper, still he was mild and courteous in his general deportment, fond of society and conversation, and universally a favorite from his great good humor and intelligence; he thought and wrote much as a

Grave of Thomas Stone at Thomas Stone National Historic Site in Port Tobacco, Maryland.

professional man, and as a statesman, on the business before him in those characters; he had no leisure for other subjects; not that he was unequal to the task, for there were few men who could commit their thought to paper with more facility or greater strength of argument. There was a severe trial of skill between the Senate and the House of Delegates, on the subject of confiscating British property. The Senate for several sessions unanimously rejected bills passed by the house of delegates for that purpose: many, very long and tart, were the messages from one to the other body, on this subject; the whole of which, were on the part of the Senate, the work of Mr. Stone, and his close friend and equal in all respects, the venerable Charles Carroll of Carrollton.

There is a Thomas Stone High School in Charles County, Maryland. Stone's signature is memorialized on a boulder at the Memorial to the 56 Signers of the Declaration of Independence in the Constitution Gardens on the National Mall in Washington, D.C. Also, in the rotunda of the National Archives, there is a large mural entitled "The Declaration" painted by Barry Faulkner depicting about half of the signers. Stone is shown standing in the very back.

Sources

Books, Magazines, Journals, Files:
Appleby, Joyce. *Inheriting the Revolution: The First Generation of Americans.* Cambridge, Massachusetts: Harvard University Press, 2000.
Atkinson, Rick. *The British Are Coming: The War for America, Lexington to Princeton, 1775-1777.* New York: Henry Holt & Co. 2019.
Bordewich, Fergus M. *The First Congress: How James Madison, George Washington, and a Group of Extraordinary Men Invented the Government.* New York: Simon and Schuster Paperbacks, 2016.
Boudreau, George W. *Independence: A Guide to Historic Philadelphia.* Yardley, Pennsylvania: Westholme Publishing, LLC. 2012.
Bowen, Catherine Drinker. *Miracle at Philadelphia: The Story of the Constitutional Convention May to September 1787.* Boston, Massachusetts: Little, Brown & Company, 1966.
Breen, T.H, *George Washington's Journey: The President Forges a New Nation.* New York: Simon & Schuster. 2016.
Chambers, II, John Whiteclay. *The Oxford Companion to American Military History.* Oxford: Oxford University Press, 1999.
Commager, Henry Steele & Richard B. Morris. *The Spirit of 'Seventy-Six: The Story of the American Revolution as Told by Participants.* New York: Harper & Rowe, 1967.
Conlin, Joseph R. *The Morrow Book of Quotations in American History.* New York: William Morrow and Company, Inc., 1984.
Daniels, Jonathan. *Ordeal of Ambition.* Garden City, New York: Doubleday & Company, Inc., 1970.
Dann, John C. *The Revolution Remembered: Eyewitness Accounts of the War for Independence.* Chicago: University of Chicago Press, 1980.
DeRose, Chris. *Founding Rivals: Madison vs. Monroe: The Bill of Rights and the Election that Saved a Nation.* New York: MJF Books, 2011.
Drury, Bob & Tom Clavin. *Valley Forge.* New York: Simon & Schuster. 2018.
Ellis, Joseph J. *Revolutionary Summer: The Birth of American Independence.* New York: Alfred A. Knopf, 2013.
———. *The Quartet: Orchestrating the Second American Revolution, 1783-1789.* New York: Alfred A. Knopf, 2015.
———. *His Excellency: George Washington.* New York: Alfred A. Knopf, 2004.
Flexner, James Thomas. *George Washington in the American Revolution, 1775-1783.* Boston: Little, Brown & Company, 1967.
Goodrich, Charles A. *Lives of the Signers of the Declaration of Independence.* Charlotteville, N.Y.: SamHar Press, 1976.

Grossman, Mark. *Encyclopedia of the Continental Congress*. Armenia, New York: Grey House Publishing, 2015.

Kiernan, Denise & Joseph D'Agnese. *Signing Their Lives Away: The Fame and Misfortune of the Men Who Signed the Declaration of Independence*. Philadelphia: Quirk Books, 2008.

———. *Signing Their Rights Away: The Fame and Misfortune of the Men Who Signed the United States Constitution*. Philadelphia: Quirk Books, 2011.

Klarman, Michael J. *The Framers' Coup: The Making of the United States Constitution*. New York: Oxford University Press, 2016.

Langguth, A. J. *Patriots*. New York: Simon and Schuster, 1988.

Larson, Edward J. *A Magnificient Catastrophe*. New York: Free Press, 2007.

Lee, Mike. *Written Out of History: The Forgotten Founders Who Fought Big Government*. New York: Penguin Books, 2017.

Lomask, Milton. *Charles Carroll and the American Revolution*. San Francisco: Ignatius Press, 2017.

Lossing, Benson J. *Pictorial Field Book of the Revolution*. New York: Harper Brothers. 1851.

Maier, Pauline. *American Scripture: Making the Declaration of Independence*. New York: Alfred A. Knopf, Inc., 1997.

Middlekauff, Robert. *The Glorious Cause: The American Revolution, 1763-1789*. Oxford: Oxford University Press, 2005.

Miller, Jr., Arthur P. & Marjorie L. Miller. *Pennsylvania Battlefields and Military Landmarks*. Mechanicsburg, Pennsylvania: Stackpole Books, 2000.

Millett, Allan R. & Peter Maslowski. *For the Common Defense: A Military History of the United States of America*. New York: The Free Press, 1984.

O'Connell, Robert L. *Revolutionary: George Washington at War*. New York: Random House. 2019.

Racove, Jack N. *Revolutionaries: A New History of the Invention of America*. New York: Houghton Mifflin Harcourt, 2011.

Raphael, Ray. *Founding Myths: Stories That Hide Our Patriotic Past*. New York: MJF Books, 2004.

Rossiter, Clinton. *1787 The Grand Convention*. New York: The Macmillan Company, 1966.

Schweikart, Larry & Michael Allen. *A Patriot's History of the United States from Columbus's Great Discovery to the War on Terror*. New York: Penguin, 2004.

Sharp, Arthur G. *Not Your Father's Founders*. Avon, Massachusetts: Adams Media, 2012.

Taafee, Stephen R. *The Philadelphia Campaign, 1777-1778*. Lawrence, Kansas: University of Kansas Press, 2003.

Wood, Gordon S. *The Radicalism of the American Revolution*. New York: Vintage Books, 1993.

———. *Empire of Liberty: A History of the Early Republic, 1789-1815*. New York: Penguin Books, 2004.

———. *Revolutionary Characters: What Made the Founders Different*. New York: Penguin Books, 2006.

SOURCES

———. *The Americanization of Benjamin Franklin.* Oxford: Oxford University Press, 2009.

Wright, Benjamin F. *The Federalist: The Famous Papers on the Principles of American Government: Alexander Hamilton, James Madison, John Jay.* New York: Metro Books, 2002.

Video Resources:

Guelzo, Allen C. *The Great Courses: America's Founding Fathers (Course N. 8525).* Chantilly, Virginia: The Teaching Company, 2017.

Online Resources:

Archives.gov – for information on the Constitutional Convention.
CauseofLiberty.blogspot.com – for information on Daniel Carroll.
ColonialHall.com – for information about the signers of the Declaration of Independence.
DSDI1776.com – for information on many Founders.
FamousAmericans.net – for information on many Founders.
FindaGrave.com – for burial information, vital statistics and obituaries.
FirstLadies.org – for information on Abigail Adams.
Newspapers.com – Hundreds of newspaper articles were accessed—too numerous to mention here.
NPS.gov – for information on various park sites.
TheHistoryJunkie.com – for information on multiple Founders.
USHistory.org – for information on multiple Founders.
Wikipedia.com – for general historical information.

Index

Adams, Abigail, 13
Adams, John, 13, 22, 35, 50, 53, 66, 68, 71, 74, 77
Adams, Samuel, 33
Addison Burial Ground, 38, 41
Alabama, 9
American Philosophical Society, 12, 70
Annapolis, Maryland, 3, 17, 19–20, 27, 29, 42, 44–45, 49, 53, 64, 67, 76, 80–83
Annapolis Tea Party, 19
Articles of Confederation, 23, 25, 32–33, 37–38, 40, 61–62, 77, 79, 82

Baldwin, Abraham, 5-9
Baldwin, Henry, 5
Baltimore, Maryland, 3, 10, 14–15, 22, 27, 30, 61, 63, 68–69, 71, 73–74, 79
Barry, John, 53
Biddle, Edward, 10-15
Biddle, Nicholas, 10
Bill of Rights, 35, 37, 77
Boston, Massachusetts, 3, 19, 39–40, 50, 58
Boston Tea Party, 19, 50
Boudinot, Elias, 41
Brown, Gustavus, Jr., 80–81
Burr, Aaron, 31

Carroll (of Carrollton), Charles, 1, 3, 16–22, 29, 84
Carroll, Daniel, 23–26, 40, 70
Carroll, John, 23
Charleston, South Carolina, 66
Chase, Samuel, 3, 18, 20, 25, 27–31, 50, 76, 77, 81
Claiborne, Maryland, 1–2, 4
Congressional Cemetery, 32, 36–37
Connecticut, 5-6, 9, 13
Continental Association, 1, 3, 10, 13, 27, 48, 50, 64, 66, 75

Deane, Silas, 13, 56, 66
Declaration of Independence, 3, 12, 16, 18, 21–23, 27, 29–30, 32–33, 37, 62, 64, 67, 75–77, 79, 82, 84
Delaware, 45, 68, 70
Delaware, University of, 69
Dickinson, John, 45
Doughoregan Manor Chapel, 16, 22

Ellicott City, Maryland, 16, 22

Few, William, 7
Fitzsimons, Thomas, 25
Forest Glen, Maryland, 23, 26
Franklin, Benjamin, 20, 29, 45, 56, 66
Frederick, Maryland, 39–40, 42, 48–49, 51–52, 80
Fredericksburg, Virginia, 53, 55

Gadsden, Christopher, 66
Galloway, James, 12–14
Georgetown University, 23
Georgia, 5–7, 9, 61–62
Georgia, University of, 5, 7, 9
Gerry, Elbridge, 32–37
Goldsborough, Robert, 3
Greene, Nathanael, 6
Gwinnett, Button, 62

Hall, Lyman, 6
Hamilton, Alexander, 25, 72, 74
Hancock, John, 21, 33
Hanson, John, 38–42
Harrison, Benjamin, 66
Harvard University, 32
Hopkins, Esek, 55
Houston, William, 7
Huntington, Samuel, 40

Jackson, James, 7
Jefferson, Thomas, 22, 25, 30–31, 55, 72
Jenifer, Daniel of St. Thomas, 43–47, 70, 79
Johnson, Thomas, 3, 48–52, 80
Johnston, Samuel, 40
Jones, John Paul, 53–60

Kościuszko, Tadeusz, 58

Lafayette, Marquis de, 68, 71, 74
Langworthy, Edward, 61–63
Lee, Arthur, 20, 56
Lee, Charles, 63
Lee, Richard Henry, 55
Lexington and Concord, 33, 66
Lynch, Thomas, 64–67
Lynch, Thomas, Jr., 64–65, 67

Madison, James, 25, 30, 32, 45, 47
Martin, Luther, 46, 70
Mason, George, 35, 45

88

INDEX

Massachusetts, 32, 35–36, 50, 66, 69
McHenry, James, 68–74
McKean, Thomas, 41
Meigs, Josiah, 7
Mercer, John Francis, 70
Middleton, Henry, 66
Mifflin, Thomas, 13–14
Monroe, James, 34
Morton, John, 13
Moultrie, William, 67
Mount Olivet Cemetery, 48, 52

New Jersey, 10, 50, 70
New York, 25, 63, 65, 70
North Carolina, 70
Notre Dame, University of, 22

Olive Branch Petition, 13, 50, 81
Oxon Hill, Maryland, 38, 41–42

Paca, William, 1, 3, 30, 75–78
Peale, Charles Willson, 76
Pendleton, Nathaniel, 7
Pennsylvania, 10–15, 45, 51, 62, 69–70, 75
Pennsylvania, University of, 75
Philadelphia, Pennsylvania, 3, 10–11, 13, 20–21, 25, 34, 40–41, 45–46, 50, 62, 66–70, 74–75, 77, 80, 82
Pickering, Timothy, 72–73
Pierce, William, 7
Port Tobacco, Maryland, 38, 43–44, 46-47, 79–80, 83

Queenstown, Maryland, 75

Randolph, Edmund, 35, 51, 70
Rock Creek Cemetery, 5, 7
Roosevelt, Theodore, 60
Ross, Betsy, 12
Ross, George, 12–13

Rush, Benjamin, 69, 75
Rutledge, Edward, 66
Rutledge, John, 66–67

St. Anne's Churchyard, 67
St. John the Evangelist Church Cemetery, 23
St. Paul's Cemetery, 27, 30–31
Savannah, Georgia, 61–62
Scull, Nicholas, 10
Sherman, Roger, 45
South Carolina, 64–67, 70
Stiles, Ezra, 6
Stone, Thomas, 44, 76, 79–84

Tallmadge, Benjamin, 73
Taney, Rogers, Brooke, 1
Tilghman, Matthew, 1–4
Tilghman, Tench, 3
Trumbull, Joseph, 13
Tubman, Harriett, 42

US Constitution, 5, 7, 16, 23, 25, 30–32, 35, 37, 43, 46, 48, 51, 68, 70–71, 74, 77–78, 84
US Naval Academy Chapel, 2, 60
US Supreme Court, 1, 5, 27, 30–31, 48, 51

Valley Forge, Pennsylvania, 21, 69
Virginia, 26, 43, 45–46, 53, 55, 70, 79

Walton, George, 7
Washington, D.C., 5, 7, 32, 36–37, 42, 47, 84
Washington, George, 3, 21, 25–26, 37, 40–42, 45, 50–51, 66–70, 72, 74, 78, 81
Wilkinson, James, 14
Willing, Thomas, 13
Wilson, James, 13
Wisconsin, 9, 47, 74

Yale College, 5–7
York, Pennsylvania, 62

www.ingramcontent.com/pod-product-compliance
Lightning Source LLC
Chambersburg PA
CBHW032148040426
42449CB00005B/439